THE TOP 100

THE TOP 100

The best baseball cards to own, ranked and rated for the collector and investor

Paul M. Green and Kit Kiefer

Bonus Books, Inc., Chicago

94   93   92   91   90   5   4   3   2   1

Library of Congress Catalog Card Number 89-82208

International Standard Book Number: 0-933893-88-4

Bonus Books, Inc.
160 East Illinois Street
Chicago, Illinois 60611

First Edition

Printed in the United States of America

Contents and List of Illustrations

• Contents •

• Contents •

Contents

Acknowledgments

Many people deserve thanks for their efforts on this book. Bob Lemke and everyone at Krause Publications deserve special mention for their encouragement and generous loan of pictures and resources.

Collector Joe Ades must be singled out for his generous loan of a number of cards from his personal collection for study and photographs. When you find cards in this book that are singled out for their rarity, thank Joe Ades for the opportunity to see them and remember the sleepless nights he put up with worrying about them while they were out on loan.

Bonus Books and its staff who encouraged us on this project and listened to every idea, no matter how unusual, deserve special thanks as well.

Kathy Winz, who somehow manages to tolerate all ideas no matter how bizarre and who then is willing to laugh when that is needed and criticize on the numerous occasions when that is required deserves her usual, but always special, thanks.

A final word of thanks must go to Kit Kiefer for his work on this project. From his first appearance at Krause Publications the general line on Kit has been that he was enormously creative and more than a bit unorthodox. Either way, he has always been terrifically entertaining and I think that shows through in this book.

Paul M. Green
Ridgeway, Wisconsin

———————

The reason I'm co-authoring this book is because when I told Paul Green he's a lousy writer and that he ought to have someone in with him who knows the difference between *it's* and *its*, he agreed and chose me. I guess he's a lousy judge of talent, too.

The story's true enough, but the sentiments are false. I have all the respect in the world for the talents and abilities of Paul Green. Paul Green knows more than anyone in the world about the microeconomics and macroeconomics of baseball cards, and the joy and art and fun of baseball cards. Those are two tough universes to keep in balance, but Paul does it somehow. So what if he mislays an apostrophe here and there? Some things are more important than grammar. Thanks, Paul. It's been an absolute pleasure working with you.

As long as I'm saying thanks, thanks also to Don Nicolay, the CEO of Krause Publications, for allowing me to do this book. Thanks to Bob Lemke, publisher of the sports division at KP, for the same. Thanks to Tom Mortenson, Don Butler, Mark Larson, Steve Ellingboe, and Jeff "Whitey" Kurowski of the KP sports staff for their assistance, and a special thanks to Larry Frank for taking the pictures you see here.

Thanks to all the people who didn't buy my first book. They forced me into an honest line of work—baseball cards.

And, for the same reason, thanks to all the companies who didn't hire me to do the jobs I thought were dull and stupid anyway. I was mad at you before, but I'm not mad at you anymore. Thanks to Dave Newman for keeping me collecting through college, and thanks to Tom DeGennaro for showing me the joy of it all, all over again. Thanks to Joe Schoeneman for his support and to Scott Kiefer for keeping all his cards Near Mint while I was beating mine into a pulp. And thanks, Mom and Dad, for buying all those cards for Scott and me over all those years. You said they'd put us through college someday. We thought you were crazy. Guess we were wrong.

Kit Kiefer
Amherst, Wisconsin

Introduction

No one buys baseball cards with the express intention of losing money. Even the most altruistic collectors have ulterior motives rattling around the back of their heads. And it's no trick to make money in baseball cards. If all you want to do is make money in baseball cards, buy unopened cases of mid-1980s cards and high-grade 1950s and 1960s cards of Hall of Famers, stick them in a vault for six months to a year, and then sell them. You'll make money—real good money. You'll beat the money-market funds and the bond market and the futures market, and if that's all that's important to you, your mission is accomplished.

But what kind of mission is that, anyway? What does it prove? And more importantly, what do you learn from it?

It's easy to figure out which cards are going to go up in value. For today's players, the daily box scores are like a stock ticker. For yesterday's players, the *Baseball Encyclopedia* doubles as a Standard & Poor's.

But the analogy is imperfect. The box scores and records report happenings after the fact. We need a crystal ball. We need to know who's going to be hot tomorrow, the day after, six months from now, a year from now. We need to know about cards with reasons for being, with directions for heading, and we'd like to know about them as soon as possible.

Perhaps these cards' reason is that they're underpriced, and their direction is up. They might be historically important or extremely rare. Most fortuitously, they could be all of the above. But they might be none of the above, and just be the cards of a player of proven and continuing popularity. Or they might represent the best in baseball-card artwork and information.

None of this stuff will make a card jump from 20¢ to $200 in six weeks. That may be the perception, but that's not even Hollywood reality. Reality is something a little more subdued, less bold, less sure. Like a dry beer in reverse. And reality is chock full of cards.

There are millions of cards out there, and our job was to pick out 100 good buys and write about them. There are a lot more than 100 good buys to write about, a fact which we as baseball-card-book writers appreciate. Some entire sets represented here by one card are great buys. Other sets and cards are simply too obscure now to merit inclusion in a book like this, but have enormous potential, assuming a market can be created for them. We can't make that assumption, however, so many caramel cards, tobacco cards, regional issues and minor-league cards are left out here. We can only comment that they remain very desirable cards that are nonetheless often extremely difficult for the average collector to sell for high prices. The ones included here are the best of a very good—and very interesting—lot.

Admittedly we have only scratched the surface of the subject of wonderful baseball cards that double as wonderful investments. But we wanted to show the hidebound collector of pre-1900 cards that there are some intriguing issues that are only a year or two old, and we wanted to show the newcomers to the hobby with little more than a few wax packs under their belts all the places they can let their collecting go.

We've rated all these cards as investments, but, in keeping with our philosophy that there's more to a card than just its investment potential, we've gone several steps beyond. Each card in this book has been rated on five different 10-point numerical scales: scarcity, marketability, historical importance, artistic value, and appreciation potential.

The scarcity scale takes into account a card's relative scarcity. No card made two years ago is going to be as scarce as a comparable card made 100 years ago. But some cards made in the 1980s are scarcer than others, just as some cards made in the 1880s are scarcer than others. T206s are more common than T213s, but a T206 Walter Johnson is more common than a T206 Honus Wagner. Our scarcity scale weighs those different factors.

As a sort of counterbalance to scarcity we have a marketability scale. Rarity is a lousy measure of investment potential. If there's only one of something in the world and only two people show interest in it, and one of them already has it, then it's a lousy investment. On the other hand, if there's 2 million of something in the world, and 4 million people want whatever it is, it's a wonderful investment. It's desirable, it's liquid, and it's ultimately exceptionally marketable.

Historical importance ought to be self-explanatory. Just realize that the baseball-card market is young. Many cards that were produced two or three years ago are extremely important in the history of the card market. This is not just an old-cards' category.

Artistic value is a subjective, Miss America sort of category, but it acknowledges what we mentioned right off the top: there ought to be more to making money in baseball cards than just making money. There are aesthetics to consider. This category considers the aesthetics.

The final category is appreciation potential, another that's self-explanatory. It's also our opinion and not written in stone. But we have faith in us and think you ought to, too.

The cards which follow may not produce a 398 percent return in the first 30 days of ownership. But they will provide their owners with a representative and ultimately important baseball-card collection. These cards are the blue chips of their respective eras. In most cases their popularity is assured. If you are going to own baseball cards, and enjoy baseball cards, and ultimately see them rise in value, what follow are the top 100 cards to own today and tomorrow.

T206
Honus Wagner

1

If you know one baseball card in the world, this is likely it. If you've been dazzled by dollar signs used in reference to a baseball card, this is probably the card that's being referred to. If you have a baseball-card want list, this card is probably at the top of that list, or buried as far down on your list as you can bury it, buried down with the other wild dreams, just so you don't get carried away with the thought of it. Some people might have you believe there are other more valuable baseball cards than this card, but there aren't. There is the T206 Honus Wagner, and then there are the rest of the baseball cards. It is the first card ever to sell for more than $100,000. It is legend. And you look at the card as carefully as you can, and you wonder why that is.

The T206 Wagner tobacco card issued in 1910 is not the rarest card in the card world. Many other cards are unique, and for many more only one or two or three examples are known. Some cards that might be the rarest, most valuable cards ever are buried away in attics or shut up in shoeboxes. This thing about the Wagner card being the hobby's most valuable is transitory. It might survive the ages; it might not.

About 40 examples of the Wagner are known, and that just might be the perfect number. Forty or so examples known means there are just enough so that one will be the subject of intense bidding every couple of years, but not so often that the selling of one will cease to be an event. And every public transaction of this card has been an event; no other cards attract such attention. Even a low-grade card, a Very Good or Good specimen, brings 'em running, and brings remarkably powerful prices. Other cards may be priced higher than a Wagner, but the prices are arbitrary. When cards are bought and sold, the Wagner always tops them all.

It's funny, but the Wagner's value is based in large part on its renown, which is based on its value. The card is valuable because it is famous; it is famous because it is valuable. It's locked into a nice circle.

The story behind the card's rarity ought to be known to every collector by now. It's part of card lore, and that doesn't hurt its value any, either. Wagner, who was an infamous stuffer and chawer of chewing tobacco, was deathly opposed to cigarettes, and supposedly demanded that the card be withdrawn when he heard of its existence. While new evidence suggests that the

Wagner-cigarette story may be on a par with the story of George Washington and the cherry tree for veracity, it still helped to popularize the card and the hobby when the card and the hobby needed all the help they could scrape together.

Better reasons for its popularity are that the card is from the T206 set, the most popular tobacco set and the most popular pre-World War I set, and that the card shows the premier shortstop of the day. Wagner is a major baseball figure, not quite on a par with Ty Cobb but equal to any other pre-Babe Ruth great, from Christy Mathewson to George Sisler to Eddie Collins. His name and the set's reputation have helped bolster the card's value.

The fact that the card comes from the T206 set can't be emphasized enough. The T206 set is beautiful and desirable, has great historical value, and is just available enough to create a tremendous liquid market for the cards.

The bottom line is that the Wagner card is the greatest rarity in perhaps the greatest baseball-card set ever.

At its current price, the T206 Wagner is no investment *per se*; at $100,000 a pop, you can't realistically expect to double your money on a Wagner in six months. But the Wagner is a different sort of investment, like a Monet or a Rembrandt. It'll bring back money, but it'll bring back attention and adulation threefold or fourfold. And for some buyers, that's far better than money.

Paul's Score: 47

Kit's Score: 42

TOTAL SCORE: 89

1934 Goudey
Lou Gehrig

2

abe Ruth had his own card set. Ted Williams had his own set, Darryl Strawberry and Don Mattingly have had their own sets, Gregg Jefferies has had a couple of sets, and even Pete Incaviglia has had his very own one-card set. All those sets vary in their disposability; none are essential. Most border on overkill. The 1934 Goudey set is the Lou Gehrig set, and it is an essential, and there is no overkill.

The '34 Goudey set has 96 cards. Eighty-seven of them feature Lou Gehrig, and 85 of those feature the Iron Horse in a supporting role. All but 12 of the cards have a small insert on the bottom quarter of the card with Gehrig's picture and the line, "Lou Gehrig says . . ." The backs have a quote from Gehrig ("by arrangement with Christy Walsh"; you decide how much of each quote is Gehrig and how much is Walsh) about the player shown on the card. The wrapper identified the set as the "Lou Gehrig Series," even though 12 of the 96 cards feature "Chuck Klein says . . ." quotes and not Gehrig.

But the wrapper was right. Gehrig is the only player in the set to appear on two cards. Babe Ruth isn't even in the set. And while there are Hall of Famers aplenty in the set—Klein, Luke Appling, Carl Hubbell, Bill Terry, Dizzy Dean, Mickey Cochrane, Charlie Gehringer, Kiki Cuyler, Jimmy Foxx, Lefty Grove, Paul Waner, Hank Greenberg, Heinie Manush, Arky Vaughan, Ernie Lombardi, and Chick Hafey—no one can stand with Ruth or Gehrig. And since there are no Ruth cards in the set, the set belongs to Gehrig by default.

There are other Lou Gehrig cards, though not that many. Another card in the '34 Goudey set, #61, is a very nice Gehrig. But no other Gehrig card, and very few cards at all, have captured a player *the way we would want him to be captured* quite the way the '34 Goudey #37 Gehrig has.

So how much value do you attach to a card's appearance in a case like this? This one card of Gehrig is the best-looking Gehrig card ever made. But should that have a major bearing on its value? Should it have any bearing at all? Well, if this were a strip card of Gehrig, and it looked like a typical strip card, it would be downgraded on value, and the common reason given would be because the card is unattractive. It ought to work in reverse. And if this were a T206 of Gehrig or a Turkey Red or a Triplefolder with Gehrig in the middle and on one side, its value would be explained away in terms of its attractiveness.

5

The card would be in demand because of its appearance. It would be liquid and easy to sell.

But in the case of the '34 Goudey Gehrig #37, the catalog consensus is that it's no more attractive than the other '34 Gehrig in the set, and therefore no more valuable. The catalog doesn't discriminate between the two Gehrig cards in the '34 set on the basis of attractiveness, because a catalog doesn't usually split those sorts of hairs. Numerical scarcity, yes. High numbers vs. low numbers, yes. But not which cards look better than other cards.

But you *can* make those determinations. At $1,800 for either Gehrig in the '34 set (that's up from $500–$550 two years ago, incidentally), you might as well go with the one that's most aesthetically pleasing. You shouldn't have any trouble finding a nice-grade example, though you will have to pay for it. Gehrig is the key card in the set, and his overall popularity is zooming. Gehrig-autographed items are in incredible demand. Still, his cards have not yet topped out. You pay a steep price for a '34 Goudey Gehrig, but there's headroom there.

That's because Gehrig stands for something. Lou Gehrig is loved and revered as a ballplayer. He deserved a set. And he deserved a card as nice as the one Goudey gave him in '34.

Paul's Score: 39

Kit's Score: 42

TOTAL SCORE: 81

1933 Goudey
Babe Ruth

vailability is no guarantee of moderate price. Unavailability is no guarantee of expense. Two pair doesn't always beat three of a kind if you're not playing poker. A Plow's Candy Nixey Callahan is $400. A '52 Topps Mickey Mantle is $6,500. A '54 Topps Ernie Banks is $600. Maybe three Plow's Candy Callahans exist, maybe fewer. That makes the Callahan about 5,000 times rarer than the Mantle, and about 10,000 times rarer than the Banks. But the prices don't reflect rarity, and they never will. They reflect demand. And that fact is just as evident when you make the comparisons less extreme and throw any rare candy card up against the key prewar gum card, the 1933 Goudey Ruth.

There are four Babe Ruth cards in the '33 Goudey set; take your pick. They're all classic examples of the Sultan of Swat. They're definitive baseball cards. If a writer who knows nothing about baseball cards asks for a card to illustrate his story, he wants a '33 Goudey Ruth. He can understand that card, and he knows his readers will understand the card. The '33 Goudey Ruth is the absolute lowest common baseball-card denominator. People who know and comprehend less than nothing about baseball and baseball cards can comprehend that player and that card.

The Ruth cards somehow catch a little of Ruth's larger-than-life presence and pin it down on cardboard. The big (for the day), colorful cards capture Ruth by showing a little more than Ruth, by showing us what we want to see and believe and calling it Babe Ruth. It's a skillfully manipulated image. Like the '52 Topps Mantle would do years later, the card uses photorealistic art to show us what we accept and think we see, and call reality.

Beyond that, the Goudeys were the first commercially successful gum cards. They were the first of the second era of baseball cards, that quick wild time between the fading away of tobacco cards and the Topps-dominated postwar renaissance. The set was one of the first big, systematically issued card sets. Nineteen thirty-three Goudeys drip historical significance.

The '33 Goudey set is complete at 240 cards, though the 240th card, Larry Lajoie (#106 in your program, and right about there in your heart), was not available until the following year, and then only if you knew it was there and asked for it. Since not many people knew it was there and fewer people asked for it, the Lajoie card is one of the hobby's classic rarities, though not a tremendously significant card otherwise. Nothing like the Ruth cards, certainly.

Collector demand for Ruth cards is tremendous, but the supply is there and prices are healthy. It's an active market. Of the four cards, #155 is easiest to find and #181 the toughest. The other two, #53 and #149, are moderately tough. Prices for the four ranged from $550–$700 two years ago. Now they're at $2,800–$3,000. Demand for Ruth and Gehrig items is feverish, so the cards may not be done moving up. The Ruth cards are keys to the '33 Goudey set, and keys to any prewar card collection. They're the first cards any dealer will look at when confronted with a '33 Goudey set, and they're the first cards you should examine when you look at a '33 Goudey set, too.

No matter what happens to the price of a classic, a classic cannot cease being a classic simply because it becomes too expensive for you to afford. You can rationalize in that direction all you want, but it won't do any good. A boattail Auburn will always be a classic car, whether it sells for $10,000 or $1.7 million. And a Goudey Ruth will always be a classic, whether it sells for $500 or $5,000. Classics never go out of style, and classics never really lose their value, either. Availability does not always mean undesirability. With the '33 Goudey Ruth, quite the opposite.

Paul's Score: 36

Kit's Score: 44

TOTAL SCORE: 80

T206 Ed Plank

PLANK, ATHLETICS AMER.

4

Any T206 that isn't pinholed and bent over backwards is a great card to own and a decent investment. But a T206 Plank is just a little greater and decenter than any card in the set, save for the Honus Wagner.

Like Honus Wagner, Eddie Plank is a Hall of Famer. Like Honus Wagner's tobacco card, the T206 Plank is one of the great rarities in baseball cards.

But unlike Wagner, Plank is not well known. He was a pitcher for the Philadelphia Athletics, and he won 327 games, more than any other lefty until Warren Spahn came along. He threw more shutouts than any other left-handed pitcher ever, and struck out more than 2,200 batters. Those numbers make a case for him being well-known, but it just ain't so.

And unlike Wagner's card, no big legend has grown up to explain the scarcity of the Plank card. The Plank card is about half as scarce as the Wagner card—about 100 survive, as compared to 50 Wagners.

There are a couple of possible explanations for the scarcity of his card. The line of type at the bottom of the card containing Plank's name and his team is often found misaligned. The cards may have fallen victim to quality control. Also, Plank may have been opposed, as Wagner is reported to have been, to having his picture included in a pack.

Because the T206 Plank is rare and any card appearance by Plank is just as rare, Plank is as popular as Wagner among Hall of Fame collectors. Even if you can't afford a T206 Plank or Wagner, other cards of these players make great investments (and wonderful party gifts).

T206 Planks were printed twice, in the 150 and 350 series, which throws doubt on the theory that Plank objected to having his likeness included in a tobacco set. His card is really more mysterious than the Wagner. But the market doesn't pay premiums for mysteries.

In fact, the market doesn't pay the premium it used to for Plank cards. The card has fallen out of favor. It used to bring 50 percent of the price of a Wagner. Now a nice Plank is lucky to bring 15 percent of a Wagner. The Plank card has been superseded by the Sherwood Magee spelling error (Magee was spelled "Magie" and then quickly corrected) among T206-rarity collectors.

The market might be right, to an extent. The Magie card is an elusive card and a true error. Its rarity is great. Plank is in an awkward spot between the ultra-rare Magie and the high-visibility Wagner.

So, given the market's attitudes and appetites, how much should a Plank card be worth?

In fairness? Not half the value of a Wagner. It's half as rare but not half as desirable. But it takes a back seat to very few other cards, period. Its current value brings it perilously close to the price of a comparable 1952 Topps Mickey Mantle, and that's wrong. The Mantle is far more common in all grades. While a Plank shouldn't be worth half a Wagner, it should be worth more than a Mantle, which suggests there's plenty of room for some major price corrections with this card. Bringing it up to 25 percent to 30 percent of a Wagner seems right in line. That would put a Wagner at $125,000, a Plank at $30,000 and a Mantle at $12,000. The price of a Plank would have to double for that to happen. Don't expect it, but do consider it. And if you have the money to spend, spend it.

Paul's Score: 39

Kit's Score: 41

TOTAL SCORE: 80

M101-4
Babe Ruth

BABE RUTH
P.—Boston Red Sox
151

ack before the blues were blue, when the good old songs were new, back in the first third of the century, rookie cards were just cards. The first card of a ballplayer held as much attraction as any card of a ballplayer, because card issues were sporadic and regional, and sometimes players would be included in a set early in their career and sometimes players would play years, great years, in the big leagues without ever once appearing on a card.

The classic case on the rookie-card point is Babe Ruth. Now suppose Babe Ruth were Babe Ruth today. A kid comes up from the Baltimore slums with a weakness for hot dogs and hot babes and hot times in the old town, and he's a fireballing pitcher. He goes 18–8 his first full year in the bigs, and the crowds just love him. The next year he's 23–12 and the next year 24–13, and the crowds just can't get enough of him.

But wait! The kid can hit, too. By his third full year he's playing the outfield some days when he isn't pitching, and by a couple years after that he hardly pitches at all. He's the original double threat. He's colorful and quotable, and the crowds just think this guy's *swell*.

What do you think would happen to his rookie card by his fourth or fifth year in the league? Would you be able to touch it with your bare hands? With asbestos gloves? With a lunar probe?

What if that rookie card wasn't in the kid's first-year set, or his second-year set? What if you had to wait until his third full year to get a card of the kid? Would you do whatever it took to get 40 or 50 or 500 or 5,000 of these cards, even if it meant eating a truckload of bread or buying a skid of magazines?

Sure. Of course you would. But that was now, and this is then. People thought differently then. The legend of Babe Ruth was barely a legend outside of Boston in 1916. There was no market in baseball cards, and certainly no particular market in the first cards of any player. Baseball cards figured little in the scheme of things. And a Babe Ruth baseball card figured a scant little more in the scheme of things than any other card.

Okay, but here it is. The M101-4 *The Sporting News* Babe Ruth card. The Babe Ruth rookie. What do you do with it? How do you approach it?

First, you have to approach it as a card from a set that was probably a much more important set when it was issued than it is now. The set consists of 200 black-and-white pictures of 1916 ballplayers. All 200 cards are known, and are numbered neatly in alphabetical order. The cards were offered as a premium by *The Sporting News*, though the same pictures were used by the Morehouse and Weil bakeries, Globe stores, and other smaller bakeries and confectioneries. All the major stars of the day are included in the set—Shoeless Joe Jackson, Ty Cobb, Honus Wagner, Connie Mack, Walter Johnson—as well as up-and-coming players like Charles Stengel and Babe Ruth. In terms of accuracy and completeness, the M101-4 set is the closest thing the decade could produce to a modern set. But today the set has few fans and even fewer rabid collectors.

The pictures in the set are black-and-white (though they are actual pictures, not fantasies, and they do have some semblance of action to them); that hurts. The cards are also small, and not the little fine-art jewels that T207s or T206s or Cracker Jack cards are. Other than that, the cards are good cards. But add to that the little matter of the Babe Ruth rookie.

The latest catalog value of the Babe Ruth rookie is $1,000. That is a lot of money; $1,000 is the dividing line between expensive and swallow-gasp-shut-your-eyes-and-pay-it expensive for most collectors. But with Mantle's not-even rookie at $6,500–$7,000 and the rookie card of Eddie Mathews—Eddie Mathews, for Pete's sake—at $1,800, what's $1,000 for a Ruth rookie?

This card is lightning in a bottle waiting to be released. It's scarce; it's one of the toughest cards to find at shows, in any condition. Its historical significance is staggering. Its catalog value in no way reflects either of these factors. If you can find one—and it could well be that many of them were snapped up on the cheap years ago by shrewd collectors—buy it. The first baseball card made of the best player ever? It is the key addition to any collection.

Paul's Score: 40

Kit's Score: 40

TOTAL SCORE: 80

1984 Donruss
Don Mattingly

The ersatz Hawaiians have a name for the 1984 Don Mattingly card. They call it "the Big Kahuna." It's the one. Accept no substitutes. Ask the man or woman who owns one. It's the card that's had the most impact on baseball cards and baseball-card collecting of any card in the history of baseball cards *from its date of issue*. The T206 Honus Wagner card has had a tremendous impact on the hobby, but its impact on other baseball cards was minimal (other than to provide the first lesson on how scarcity equals value), and its immediate impact was no impact at all, because collectors of that day didn't grasp the dynamics of the Honus Wagner card situation. They didn't drive up the price of the Honus Wagner card, because there was no price to drive up. Similarly, the '52 Topps Mickey Mantle is a great card, the hobby version of the Great Pyramid of Cheops, but collectors didn't clamor especially hard for Mickey Mantle cards in 1952. It was five to 10 years before a demand market developed for Mickey Mantle cards. With Don Mattingly cards the demand market existed virtually from day one.

The 1984 Donruss Don Mattingly acted as a lightning rod, attracting every bit of demand for any baseball cards at all right to it. It's easy to see now that it was the perfect card at the perfect time. It was relatively scarce at a time when relative scarcity was not known. For their first three years in business Donruss and Fleer tried to keep their production up with Topps. Donruss was common, Fleer was common, Topps was common. All of a sudden in 1984 Donruss wasn't as common anymore.

No one knows how scarce '84 Donruss cards are in comparison to '84 Fleer and Topps cards. Fewer cards were made, that's for sure. They are not real scarcities—not the way we define scarcities, anyway. But for a time in 1984 there was a *perceived* scarcity, a chasm of availability between Donruss over there and Fleer and Topps over here. And the symbol of that scarcity was our Don Mattingly card.

Mattingly was perfect for generating scarcity because he was a New York Yankee who hit home runs. His cards had a tremendous built-in demand. When he started hitting home runs and everything else in 1984 (he finished with 23 home runs, 110 runs batted in, 207 hits, 44 doubles, and a .343 average), that demand came out and demanded his cards, right away, money no object. Well, the only Mattingly cards to buy were the 1984 Topps, Fleer and Donruss Mattinglys. Topps was okay, Fleer was okay, but Donruss was supposedly in shorter supply than the other two. So naturally people wanted Donruss Don Mattinglys, and naturally, the price for Donruss Mattinglys went up. That price rise attracted more people, who bought more Donruss Mattinglys, and the price went up again. That attracted still more people, who bought still more Donruss Mattinglys, and the price went up again, and more people bought Donruss Mattinglys, and by this time there *was* a shortage of Donruss Mattinglys. But it was not a supply shortage; it was a *demand* shortage, caused by excessive demand above an adequate supply. That's the best kind of shortage, and that was the signal that baseball cards had outgrown the mere hobby stage and had reached the gangly, awkward stage where prices go up for no real good reason and people want things, buy things, and then forget why they wanted them.

We owe this to the Donruss Don Mattingly card. It singlehandedly established the rookie-based card-speculation market, put money in the pockets of dealers, put great big chunks of money in the pockets of all the card companies, brought more card companies into the market, brought hundreds of thousands of collectors into the market, and indirectly provided the proper environment for the development of mega-autograph shows, investment portfolios and card-grading services. Anything that's present in the card market now that wasn't present before 1984 can be traced in some way to the Donruss Don Mattingly card.

Does that mean you should buy the '84 Donruss Don Mattingly card? Depends on how much of a historian you are. It is expensive ($65 and holding), but never underestimate the ability of a New York slugger's baseball card to go up in value, even if it has to swim upstream to do it. In terms of appreciation, it's not the best card you can buy, but look at it this way: if it wasn't for the '84 Donruss Don Mattingly there wouldn't be such a thing as card appreciation. So you probably ought to buy this card.

Paul's Score: 39

Kit's Score: 40

TOTAL SCORE: 79

1914 Cracker Jack
Joe Jackson

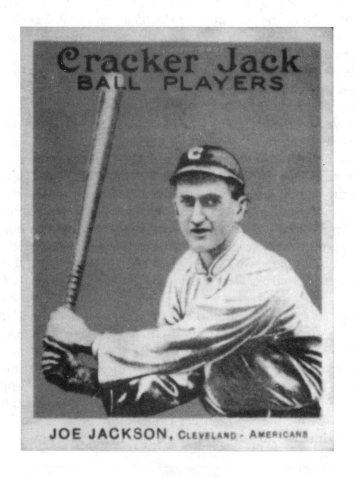

7

ow do you explain Joe Jackson to someone who's never heard of Joe Jackson? How do you explain a ballplayer who could barely read or write getting caught up, wittingly or unwittingly, in a gambling scandal, and then being banned from baseball for life on a flimsy mess of evidence? How do you explain the tragedy of one of the greatest players ever to put 'em on having to take 'em off at the height of his career and then spend the rest of his life trying awkwardly to clear his name?

You can start with Pete Rose and draw a few parallels, but the tragedy of Joe Jackson has deeper proportions. Joe Jackson stood accused of trying to throw a World Series in which he hit .375 with a home run and six runs batted in, fielded flawlessly and ran the bases with his usual abandon. Judge Kenesaw Mountain Landis threw him and seven others out of baseball and figured that would be it, but that was far from it. The judge couldn't take Joe Jackson out of baseball. Jackson is more a part of baseball now than he ever was when he was playing.

It's curious how Joe Jackson has developed into baseball's cross between Elvis Presley and James Dean and how his legend has grown after his banning and after his death. The movie *Eight Men Out* supported his claim; the book *Shoeless Joe* and the movie *Field Of Dreams* supplied the poetry. Jackson is better known than most members of baseball's Hall of Fame, and he's famous because he's not allowed in it.

Jackson's fame has boosted the price of his cards to the point where they are priced on a level with the cards of Gehrig, Cobb and Ruth as the most expensive prewar cards of all.

The least expensive Joe Jackson card is a Play Ball card produced long after Judge Landis made his pronouncement. To a true Jackson fanatic (and there are plenty of them, more than pure Cobb fanatics and almost as many as pure Ruth or Gehrig fanatics), the only attractions of the 1940 Play Ball are its price—hundreds of dollars, as opposed to thousands—and the fact that it identifies him as "Shoeless Joe" Jackson.

The other Joe Jackson cards are some obscure, homely strip cards, an E90–1 American Caramel card, and two others. The caramel card is relatively attractive and sought-after, but the most popular Joe Jackson cards are the 1914–15 Cracker Jack Jacksons.

Cracker Jacks are fun, fascinating cards, tremendously attractive things that look exactly the way a card issued in the early 1900s ought to look. Like almost every card of that era, Cracker Jacks are scarce and susceptible to plagues, and just about impossible to find in high grades. The particular plague that affects Cracker Jacks is staining. These cards were placed in boxes of candy in 1914. Storage being what it was back then, and air conditioning being some cold, wild dream, and Cracker Jack being Cracker Jack, the cards picked up sugar and oil and syrup from the confection. Unstained 1915 Cracker Jacks are next to impossible to find. Unstained 1914 Cracker Jacks are impossible.

Well, not necessarily impossible. But it will take a minor miracle to find a 1914 Cracker Jack Jackson that somehow escaped candy staining and has been carefully handled and well treated for 75 years.

Despite the odds, there are still a few nice Joe Jacksons around. The big money—$2,000 and up for a 1914, $1,900 and up for a 1915 (up from $800 and $700 respectively two years ago)—does bring them out. Even so, you may have to wait years to find one and then have to face the prospect of cleaning out the savings account just to get it home. But it's worth it. The card's gone up 25 percent in the last two years, and it's not going to stop going up. Not as long as the Joe Jackson mystique remains, anyhow.

Paul's Score: 38

Kit's Score: 40

TOTAL SCORE: 78

1952 Topps Mantle

8

There's a very simple way of stating exactly what this card has done for the baseball-card hobby. Without it the hobby would have this:

We could go on like that, but you might get to like it.

But do you get it? If there hadn't been a 1952 Topps Mantle, there wouldn't have been a baseball-card hobby like the one we have. There wouldn't be 1986 Donruss Cansecos or Fleer Update Goodens. There probably wouldn't even be Donruss and Fleer. There might be tobacco cards, but no one fully behind the wheel of his gray matter would consider paying $100,000 for a T206 Honus Wagner. Without the '52 Topps Mantle there wouldn't be price guides to follow the ever-changing prices because prices wouldn't be ever-changing, and there certainly wouldn't be this book and we certainly wouldn't be getting any money, and we had better stop this thing before it gets too depressing.

But it's true. The 1952 Topps Mickey Mantle, for whatever reason, be it racial or emotional or intellectual or financial, is the icon for a generation of card collectors. More than a generation; a generation and a half at least, and maybe two full generations. For people who have it its worth far exceeds its value, and considering its value can run up towards $10,000 that's an awful powerful statement.

Yeah, but this is an awful powerful card. It brought 35-year-old stockbrokers and market researchers and ophthalmologists and assembly-line workers into the baseball-card market when nothing else was doing that and there wasn't a baseball-card market *per se*, just a bunch of Peter Pans with shoeboxes and grown-up Little League shortstops with paunches and sweet memories. Just about anyone who collected cards as a kid in the 1950s wanted the Mantle card first when he came back to cards 25 and 30 years later. As more of these ex-kids looked for and bought this card, the price of the card increased. Other adults saw this and bought more Mantle cards as a speculative invest-ment, and more '52 Topps cards, and more '53 Bowmans, and more baseball cards period. One thing led to another and another and two more over there in the corner, and all of a sudden Sly Stone was right: there *was* a riot goin' on here, and it was over baseball cards of all things. And we owe it all to the '52 Topps Mantle.

A '52 Topps Mantle is a lousy investment. Sure, there's absolutely no downside risk, and it'll probably inch up in value closer to the $10,000 mark over the next few years, but an unopened wax case of '87 Topps will give you five times the appreciation with a tenth of the fanfare. The '52 Mantle is a card to buy to have and look at, and if you buy one to stick it in a bank vault you'd better be good and able to account for your actions. It's the symbol of an era, a hobby and an industry. It's about as big as the American flag. Buy one, and display it proudly.

Paul's Score: 33

Kit's Score: 44

TOTAL SCORE: 77

1953 Topps
Satchel (Satchell)
Paige

You're adults, or if you're not adults you're pretty smart kids. You don't need a history lesson on the Negro leagues.

But maybe you do. Some of the greatest players in baseball played in the Negro leagues. They traveled from hick-town doubleheaders to minstrel-show exhibition games to anything-goes league games crammed into Grapes of Wrath autograph-model cars and buses. Some of the leagues' stars have familiar names: Satchel Paige, Jackie Robinson, Larry Doby, Monte Irvin, Roy Campanella. Some have names that may ring a more distant bell: Cool Papa Bell, Josh Gibson, Buck Leonard, Ray Dandridge. But the names of some of the players—such great names, such great players—are lost as to where and when and how great they played. If only Leon Day and John Henry Lloyd, the "black Wagner," and Smokey Joe Williams, the contemporary—and some say the equal—of Walter Johnson, and Martin Dihigo and Christobel Torriente could have played where they should have played.

But they didn't, and Satchel Paige did. Paige was by all accounts the best pitcher in the history of the Negro leagues, and that's about the only thing all accounts agree on with Satchel Paige. There's no agreement on his date of birth or how many games he won in the Negro leagues, or how his arm rejuvenated itself in the late 1930s, or how he learned to throw the mysterious stuff he brought to the Cleveland Indians in 1948. They told Bill Veeck he was washed up then, but Paige won six games and lost only one down the stretch and helped lead the Cleveland Indians to the pennant.

Satchel Paige finally showed up on a baseball card after that. It's a 1949 Bowman, and it's priced at $1,100, not because it's unusually attractive or anything but because it's ostensibly his rookie card. Rookie card? Of a pitcher who had pitched against Dizzy Dean and Bob Feller—and won—for the better part of 20 years? What a conceit. The 1949 Bowman Paige is no more his rookie card than the 1953 Topps card is his rookie card. And the '53 Topps is much better looking and a whole lot cheaper besides.

How much cheaper? Satchel Paige's '53 Topps card (misspelled "Satchell") catalogs at $325 in top grade. That's still plenty of money for a '53 Topps card in that number series; Whitey Ford brings $90 and Ralph Kiner $50. But Satchel Paige isn't Ralph Kiner or Whitey Ford, or even Roy Campanella or Jackie Robinson. He is one, unique, an ageless, enigmatic pitching version of Babe Ruth crossed by Casey Stengel. Charisma? Paige oozed it. Symbolism? Paige ran it through his hair like pomade. You can buy Kiner cards and Ford cards any day of the week. But Paige is, was and will always be something special.

And for proof, here are Paige's six rules for staying young, just as he set them down 20 or 30 or 70 years ago:

1. Avoid fried meats, which angry up the blood.

2. If your stomach disputes you, lie down and pacify it with cool thoughts.

3. Keep the juices flowing by jangling around gently as you move.

4. Go very light on the vices, such as carrying on in society. The social ramble ain't restful.

5. Avoid running at all times.

6. Don't look back. Something might be gaining on you.

That's why you want to have his card. Thanks, Satch.

Paul's Score:	38
Kit's Score:	39
TOTAL SCORE:	77

1975 Topps Mini
George Brett

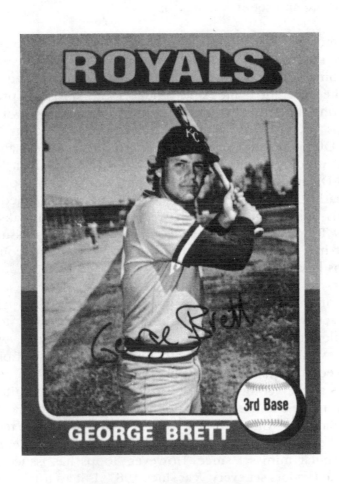

10

The people at Topps are always thinking up new ways to combine their two products: bubble gum and pictures of athletes. Sometimes the ways they think up to combine the two are pure genius. Topps' Big Baseball set, a three-series set of glossy, flashy cards designed specifically for the three months when kids are out of school, is a splendidly executed set with a brilliant marketing concept behind it. Same with Topps' sticker-cards and its Traded set and its Tiffany set. Each one is the product of a company that isn't afraid to throw something new out there and see if it'll sink or sail.

But most of Topps' bright ideas sink. Most of everyone's bright ideas sink in business, and more consumer items sink than anything. If they didn't, it would take five supermarkets to hold all the different brands and products and spins off products, and one supermarket alone to handle pot-scrubbers with soap. Topps' Candy Lids sunk. Its Scratch-Offs sunk, as did its Rub-Offs and Rub-Downs and Tattoos and transfers and Peel-Offs and decals and cloth stickers and Action All-Star Stickers. Its 3-D cards sunk two years running, and so did its plaks and an earlier batch of 3-D cards and a new issue called Topps Heads-Ups that are a cross between 3-D cards and plaks. Since 1949 Topps has tried out about 70 one-year or test issues, and all it has to show for it are some glossy sets and coins. But Topps keeps trying. It has to.

One of Topps' most mystifying test issues is its 1975 mini set. The set was issued primarily in Michigan, ostensibly to see if people would notice smaller cards, and if they did, whether they would equate them with nuclear holocaust. Collectors noticed the smaller cards right off, and bought up as many packs as they could find—which turned out to be quite a few. As scarce test issues go, this one was fairly common, and fairly popular. But from Topps' perspective, the immediate test must have been a failure; there was no '76 mini set, and there's been no regular mini set since. However, Topps has issued a Mini League Leaders set every year since 1987. Is it an offshoot of the '75 Mini set? Quite possibly. It's not illogical.

The one-off '75 Mini set remains a collector favorite. The cards are dainty and cute and clever and attractive, much more attractive than the regular '75s (which rank low on most folks' attractiveness scales). The set goes for $850, up from $650 two years previous. It's $300 more than the regular '75 set, and the gap between the two sets is widening some. The key card in both sets is the George Brett rookie, and it's more key in the Mini set than it is in the regular set.

Brett's a career .300 hitter with one Most Valuable Player award to his credit, a World Series ring, and a high profile. Brett remains an exceptionally popular and productive player; based on his numbers at this stage of his career, Brett is a certain Hall of Famer. His mark has already been made.

Given those givens, $70 is a cheap price for Brett's '75 Mini, especially since a non-rookie card of Mike Schmidt goes for $60 in the same set, and a Pete Rose card goes for $40. Brett's card has more than doubled in the last two years, and as a Hall of Fame premium starts being built into his cards, that price will rise nicely over the next several years.

While the Topps Mini set may have been the great idea that failed, the '75 Mini Brett remains the great idea that didn't.

Paul's Score: 38

Kit's Score: 38

TOTAL SCORE: 76

1954 Bowman
Ted Williams

11

Topps and Bowman, back before they were just the baseball-card equivalent of Busch and Bud, were mortal enemies. Topps would steal players from Bowman, and Bowman would steal them back. Some players signed contracts with one and not the other, and then broke their contracts with the one and signed with the other, leaving blank spaces in the set. You think Topps numbered its 274-card 1953 set to 280 on purpose?

(That's not as outlandish as it sounds. Card companies have never been above putting more numbers than cards in a set as a ploy to get kids to buy more packs to fill in their missing numbers.)

Some players didn't sign with either Topps or Bowman. Stan Musial didn't appear on a card from 1954 to 1958. And Ted Williams was, as you might expect, contrary.

Ted Williams didn't appear on baseball cards in 1952 or 1953. While that fact is made easier to take by the knowledge that he only appeared in 43 games those two years, Teddy Thumper Ballgame remained one of the game's top stars, and either Topps or Bowman would have stolen cigarettes from a biker bar to get Williams in their card sets either year.

Bowman was the last company to have Williams in a card set, in 1951, and they prevailed again in 1954 when Williams appeared as card #66, right next to Mickey Mantle.

But Ted Williams will be, and was, Ted Williams. The arrangement didn't last. For reasons that still aren't completely clear, Williams opted out of the set halfway through the set's press run. A pleasant, low-key card of the pleasant, low-key Jimmy Piersall was hastily made up and inserted in Williams' place. The result was one of the most significant pull-and-replace situations since Wagner and Lajoie.

Anytime a player is pulled from a set and replaced with another player, or another version of the same player, collectors should get their head out of the Gravy Train and take note. In the case of the '54 Bowman Williams they might even want to wipe their mouths.

The card's a monster, a beast. You can't find it in top grades. You can barely find it at all. Its current value, $2,200, is still $1,650 more than anything else in the '54 Bowman set, but for a truly scarce card of Ted Williams, who appears in sets in the '50s about as often as the Felt Pennants Checklist, it's just red-clay cheap.

The '54 Williams has nearly tripled in value in the last two years, but that's just average for early 1950s cards of Hall of Famers. There's still headroom for this card. Error-and-variation freaks have to have it, because it's the most significant error of the 1950s. Red Sox fans, bless their masochistic ground-ball-through-the-legs souls, have to have it because it's Ted. And we want it because we know how scarce it is.

The baseball-card error market tends to be a little freaky. Not this card. This card will always be good.

Paul's Score: 37

Kit's Score: 39

TOTAL SCORE: 76

1951 Bowman
Mantle

12

It's impossible for you to buy a Mickey Mantle card and be wrong, as far as intent is concerned. You might get misled on the grade or buy a reprint by mistake (shame, shame, shame—being informed is your best weapon), but at least your heart is in the right place. It's even more impossible to keep a few Mantle cards from creeping into your collection. If you collect baseball cards for the gentle way they reflect baseball, you have to have a Mickey Mantle card or two in your collection because Mantle is the symbol for a magnificent era of baseball. If you collect baseball cards because you like the way they look, you have to have a couple of Mantles because Mantle never really took a bad baseball-card picture or had a bad likeness reproduced. If you collect cards for the investment potential, you have to have a few Mickey Mantle cards in your baseball-card portfolio—how we do hate that word—because over the long term nothing holds its value better than a properly graded, high-grade Mickey Mantle card.

And as long as you're filling your collection or portfolio or whatever with Mantle cards you might as well set the '51 Bowman Mantle right up front, because it's the pappy of them all. Mantle's true rookie card isn't his most valuable—yet—but the gap between it and the '52 Topps continues to narrow. While the Topps Mantle has stabilized at $7,000 or so, the '51 Bowman Mantle has moved up to the $4,800–$5,000 neighborhood in a big hurry.

Aesthetically, the card's a pleasure. Mantle never looked younger—naturally—or more eager to take on a decade of long home runs and spectacular catches and knee injuries and heavy drinking with Billy Martin. It benefits from showing up in a set where there are almost no unforgivable artistic clinkers. Symbolically, what could be better than the rookie card of the most important player of baseball's halcyon days? And economically, while the card has retrenched just a little in recent months, remember that it made a move from $2,000 to $5,000 in 14 months, and a move from $900 in a little more than two years. It's a correction in the market, but the correction's over and this card is set to move back up again.

How much? Not much over the short term. The market's still trying to figure out the proper distance between the '51 Bowman Mantle and the '52 Topps Mantle. But over the long term Mantle cards will always outperform the market in terms of price performance and liquidity. And if you're going to start with Mantle cards you have to start here.

Paul's Score: 33

Kit's Score: 43

TOTAL SCORE: 76

1941 Play Ball
Pee Wee Reese

"PEE WEE" REESE

13

W hy isn't that card $1,000?'' dealer Brian Goldner asked.

He was talking about the 1941 Play Ball Pee Wee Reese, and it's a good question. The card certainly has a lot of things going for it. But $1,000 worth of things? Maybe.

Start with the player. How much is Pee Wee Reese worth now? How much was he worth to the Dodgers through the 1940s and 1950s? He was worth six pennants and one World Series crown. He anchored the Dodgers' middle infield, playing with the poise of an on-the-field manager. He was a clutch hitter, a lifetime .269 hitter with a .366 on-base percentage. And maybe the most important thing he did was ease the transition for Jackie Robinson from the Negro leagues to the major leagues.

Pee Wee Reese came from Kentucky. He could have fought Robinson's promotion to the Dodgers and made things miserable for Robinson, perhaps even postponed the integration of major-league baseball for years. But Reese didn't fight it. He stood with Robinson, and together they cemented the most diverse baseball club ever to step on a diamond to that time, and turned that club into a family. You think Tommy Lasorda's schtick about the Dodger family and bleeding Dodger blue is an act? Lasorda learned his Dodgerisms at Pee Wee Reese's knee. No one beefed much when Reese was elected to the Hall of Fame. The very strong consensus was he deserved it.

His '41 Play Ball card is pretty strong, too. It's Reese's rookie card, and unlike many rookie cards of 1950s ballplayers, this card could stand its ground in any baseball-card art contest any day.

It's expensive for that reason and others. It was one of the last cards issued before World War II, and many of its kind went off to the wartime scrap-paper drives. Uncle Sam appreciated it back then, but we're not too thrilled about it today.

Play Balls must have been particular favorites of the scrap drives, because, as Goldner said, "I've been noticing lately that you can find top-grade Goudey commons, but nobody seems to have more than one or two Play Ball commons.''

The set is taken for granted. People like the '41 Play Ball set, and they expect the cards to be there. But the cards aren't there—at least, not in the quantities people expect, and especially not in Near Mint or better grades.

The '41 Play Ball Reese is also a high number. All '41 Play Balls from #49 up are considered to be high numbers, and they're all scarce, and rare in high grades.

We may not perceive the '41 Play Ball Reese as being much different from the key rookie cards of the early '50s. But it is. It's a product of a different time and different sets. It's soared in price in the last two years, but only to $700. There ought to be more of a jump for this card. Perhaps there will be next year or the year after. It'll come sometime.

Paul's Score: 38

Kit's Score: 38

TOTAL SCORE: 76

T-3 Turkey Red
(Vic Willis)

WILLIS, PITTSBURG
NOW WITH ST. LOUIS NAT'L.

14

Which Turkey Red? Heck; any of them. It doesn't matter. We chose Vic Willis, but it could just as easily have been a Hall of Famer like Christy Mathewson or John McGraw or Ty Cobb or Nap Lajoie or Cy Young or Hughie Jennings or Addie Joss or Roger Bresnahan or Wee Willie Keeler or Johnny Evers. They're all wonderful. From whatever perspective you choose to look at them, they're wonderful. In fact, they're so wonderful one dealer we know who has sold a lot of them through the years said the other day, "That's it. I'm not going to sell any more nice Turkey Reds."

All the more to keep to himself. And with Turkey Reds the temptation is to keep them all to yourself. Cards this handsome, this scarce, this affordable and this good an investment shouldn't be shared.

Turkey Reds are cabinet cards. There's some confusion over that term, but it's really straightforward. A cabinet card is what it says—a card meant to be displayed in a glass-front curio cabinet, the way you might display a ceramic waxwing or a "Souvenir Of Lead, S.D." ashtray. Cabinet cards are large, too; Turkey Reds measure 5¾ inches by 8 inches. Mark that off on a piece of paper and you'll see how Turkey Reds dwarf other cards, especially tobacco cards.

The Turkey Reds were given away as a premium in 1911. When you mailed in 10 coupons from Turkey Red cigarettes or 25 coupons from Old Mill or Fez cigarettes, you got to choose your premium picture from 100 baseball players or 25 boxers.

Do a little figuring and you'll come up with 1,000 Turkey Red coupons needed to complete a set, and 2,500 Old Mill or Fez coupons. Completing a set would have cost a lot of money back then—$100, assuming cigarette packs cost 10 cents—and would have been a darn sight more hazardous to your health than chewing bubble gum. Turkey Red was not a low-tar brand; neither were Old Mill or Fez. You could have completed your Turkey Red set for a lot less than the $125 per common the cards go for today, but you probably wouldn't have lived long enough to enjoy it.

Turkey Reds aren't common; no cabinet cards ever were. It cost too much in the form of time, effort expended and money to get them. Turkey Reds are beyond uncommon; they're beautiful. If you were to take a poll among collectors who have seen

Turkey Reds, Diamond Stars, Goudeys, tobacco cards, '52 Topps cards, and Upper Deck cards, and you were to ask them which issue they thought was prettiest of all time, the majority would answer Turkey Reds. Everything else would be fighting it out for second place. It wouldn't even be close.

Turkey Reds cost $125 for commons, like this Vic Willis card. Second-echelon Hall of Famers like Joss and Jennings and Keeler cost $225–$350. Cards of the best of the best— Mathewson, Cobb, Young—get closer to $1,000 every day.

But Willis is a cut above the common Turkey Red, even if he's priced with the commons. First of all, there's a Willis variation. His team name is given as "Pittsburg and St. Louis" or just "Pittsburg." The "Pittsburg" variation is $125; the "Pittsburg and St. Louis" variation is $225.

And then there's the possibility that Vic Willis might make the Hall of Fame. Sure; Cooperstown isn't done with the pre-1920 crowd just yet. There's Bill Dahlen and Mike Mitchell and Willis, all with a shot through the Veterans' Committee. Willis finished his career with a big 247–205 won-lost record. His 247 wins are the most by any old-time pitcher who isn't in the Hall of Fame. Word is that Willis just missed election in the committee's last round of voting. Another round, and the voting going for Willis this time, and his regular card—which doesn't have any Cooperstown cushion built into its value—will jump $100 overnight. There's no telling where his error card might end up.

As with any card, condition's the key with Turkey Reds. Try to find one that hasn't been pinholed (everybody, it seems, wanted their cabinet cards stuck to the wall). Try to find one with solid corners. Try to find a clean one. But if that doesn't work, remember that lower-grade T-3s are still the prettiest low-grade cards that ever were.

Save your money for one T-3, and seriously consider Vic Willis. You won't lose, and you could face the possibility of winning in a big way.

Paul's Score: 36

Kit's Score: 39

TOTAL SCORE: 75

1968 Topps
Nolan Ryan/
Jerry Koosman

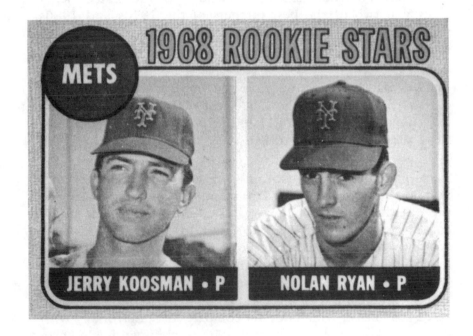

15

There are only a few baseball cards you could call meaningful with a straight face. Attractive? Yes. Informative? Sometimes. Unusual? You bet. Meaning*less?* Darn right. Overpriced, useless and ugly as sin on a Saturday night? All the time. But not meaningful. Not hardly ever meaningful.

Maybe one card a decade can qualify as being meaningful, meaning more than a dollar sign or a heartbeat of nostalgia to someone. As far as the 1960s go, the 1968 Ryan/Koosman card is *the* card—not necessarily the meaning of life, but close. It gives you two of the best pitchers of the 1970s and 1980s making their very first baseball-card appearance on the very same card and in New York uniforms.

The best part is that neither Koosman nor Ryan spent that much of his career in New York. So you get all the New York inflationary push on the one hand without having a card of true New York players on the other.

Ryan you know all about. Career strikeout leader, career won-lost record in the 270–250 range. The pitching version of the one-dimensional ballplayer. But Koosman's career might come as a little bit of a shock to you. Koos won 20 games once with the Mets and once with the Twins. He also pitched with a lot of teams where he gave up three runs a game, and that was just enough to lose, so he has a few big losing seasons to go along with the big winning seasons. He finished his career with a 222–209 mark, which doesn't compare that unfavorably with Ryan's mark. And Koos did most of his pitching with a left arm that was about one-quarter arm and three-quarters pain. Koos was a gamer.

Koos will probably never make the Hall of Fame, though. Ryan will. So the most meaningful card of the decade shows one Hall of Famer and one pretty good pitcher, two members of the 1969 "Miracle Mets," the Brooklyn Dodgers of the 1960s. For that you pay $725.

Is it worth it? The card keeps rising in price as Ryan keeps striking out batters. That makes it worth it. In comparison to some of the undervalued cards you could buy for $725 it's not worth it, but our opinion is all that makes those undervalued cards undervalued. The Ryan-Koosman card is a well-known quantity. It's no big secret. It's just a great baseball card.

For some collectors the sight of this card is just a little too much to bear. They break down, they rend their garments, they speak in tongues. It's not necessary that you do any of that. But a little gnashing of teeth for the Koos might be nice.

Paul's Score: 41

Kit's Score: 34

TOTAL SCORE: 75

E90-1 Mike Mitchell

Mitchell, r. f. Cincinnati.

16

The Mike Mitchell E90-1 is like a blockbuster movie that's about to arrive at your neighborhood theater. It may go belly up there, but from the looks of things, it's going to have them lining up around the block as soon as word gets out that it's on the way.

Early candy and gum cards—the real early stuff, before Goudey and Gum, Inc.—are terrifically underappreciated. They're contemporaries of the early tobacco issues, the T205s and such, but while the tobacco issues get all the press and collectors, the early candy and gum issues—the "E" cards—get pushed over to one side.

T cards and E cards have more in common than not. They're about the same size, and look alike. They're usually in color, and almost always quite attractive. The sets of both are usually quite large.

But the E scts often have players T sets don't have, players like Honus Wagner and Shoeless Joe Jackson. And since the candy cards were printed on thinner stock to start with and then usually handled by children, they're quite a bit harder to find in good shape than nice T cards. No wonder one dealer said, "I sell the tobacco cards, but nice E cards go into my collection."

Which is probably where all the nice E cards are. They certainly aren't on dealers' tables for sale.

The E90-1 set is the T206 set of E cards. If that analogy still leaves you a little mystified, try this: The E90-1 set is the biggest E-card set, and the most difficult to complete. Collectors who have their T206 set done down to the Wagner card are still working on their E90-1 set. And are still a long ways from completing it.

The E90-1 set has its big-name players and rare cards, too. Where the T206 set has Wagner and Mathewson and Plank and Magie and Wagner, the E90-1 has a horizontal-format Wee Willie Keeler, Tris Speaker and Ed Walsh, and rarities like Sweeney and Peaches Graham. Those are cards that are tough to find in any condition at any price. And then there's Mike Mitchell of Cincinnati.

The Mike Mitchell E90-1 is rare. We don't know exactly how rare. But one dealer called it "the Honus Wagner of E cards," and another dealer, David Festberg, said, "You can quote me on the Mitchell. It's the Wagner of E cards. It's the toughest. That's it. I've had two Mitchells, and only one Wagner, in my life."

Does that mean the Mitchell is twice as common as the Wagner? Oh, probably not. But the Mitchell is a very, very special card.

Not always that valuable, though. There was a Mitchell in last year's Alan Rosen auction, and it sold for $3,000. That may break all sales records for Mitchell cards, but in the scheme of things, with Wagners up there in the six figures, it's modest. A two-bedroom ranch in the suburbs, as these things go.

Certainly Mike Mitchell, a career .278 hitter through eight major-league seasons, was no Honus Wagner. Nor does his card have a fascinating—if somewhat dubious—story behind it. Those factors could help make his card less valuable. But they can't and shouldn't account for his card only carrying a $2,000 catalog value in top grade, or a $1,000 value in Excellent, or a $600 value in Very Good. Those prices have to be adjusted upward, and will be, if and when E cards get the attention they deserve. As Festberg said, "With all the new strength in the hobby and how knowledgeable people are getting, it's amazing that E cards are still being overlooked." Overlooked now. Not forever.

Paul's Score: 39

Kit's Score: 36

TOTAL SCORE: 75

1952 Topps Mays

17

ere's a concept straight out of the statistics book for you to consider when looking at cards from the 1952 Topps set: unweighted or corrected value. It's boring as an ice auger, but it'll help give you a much better idea of what's worth what, and where a '52 Topps Willie Mays fits in.

The '52 Topps Mays is the forgotten man in a run of Hall of Famers that stretches from 246 to 407 in that classic set. George Kell, Bob Lemon, Early Wynn, Mickey Mantle, Jackie Robinson, Roy Campanella, Pee Wee Reese, Hoyt Wilhelm, Billy Herman, Bill Dickey, and Ed Mathews show up in the run. Values range from $150 for Wynn and Lemon to $6,500 for Mantle. Mays fits in fourth, behind Mantle, Mathews and Campanella.

You'll also find four distinct high-number series and four sets of values within this run. Cards from 251–280 and 301–310 are the most common, cards from 281–300 are slightly scarcer, and cards from 311–407 are three times scarcer than that.

The idea between corrected value is to state the values of all these Hall of Famers' cards in terms of the *least* valuable cards in the series.

Here's how it works: Early Wynn's card is valued at $150, and it's in the 251–280 series where commons are worth $40. The corrected value of his card is $50, same as its list value. Hoyt Wilhelm, on the other hand, has his card—his rookie card—in the very scarce 311–407 series, where common prices are three and three-quarters times those in the 251–280 series. It's a $400 card, but when you correct for the series Wilhelm's card has a value of $130.

The uncorrected values of Hall of Famers' cards in the high-number series of the '52 Topps set run like this (from least expensive to most expensive): Lemon, Wynn, Herman, Wilhelm, Reese, Dickey, Robinson, Mays, Campanella, Mathews, Mantle. But when you take out the high-number bias the order goes like this: Herman, Wilhelm, Lemon, Wynn, Reese, Dickey, Robinson, Campanella, Mathews, Mays, Mantle. The gap between Mantle and Mays is still there, but at least it's not as large.

The point is that Mays' card holds its value. It holds its value in relation to cards of other Hall of Famers in the '52 Topps set, and it more than holds its value compared to other cards. The only difference between the Mays '52 Topps card and, say, the

Campanella is that you're not forced to pay for the value up front because of high-number scarcity.

Normally the recommendation with '52 Topps is to go with scarcity, buy the high numbers in the best condition possible, sell all your major appliances and apply for a charge account at the Salvation Army. But Mays is a special case. His card has kept a consistent value to the point of being undervalued; it's gone from $700 to $950 in the last two years, while the set has moved from $22,000 to $38,000. It stands for quite a bit, though, and it's a wonderful card. When you throw out all the numbers, that's what important.

Paul's Score: 33

Kit's Score: 40

TOTAL SCORE: 73

1934–35 Diamond Stars Jimmie Foxx

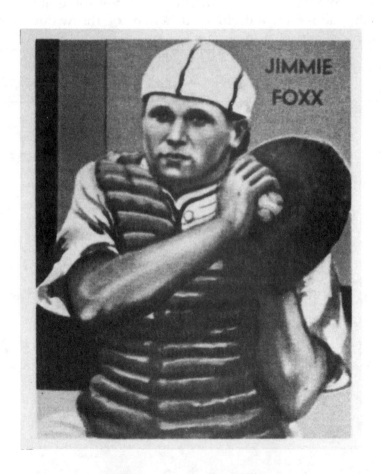

18

Jimmie Foxx a catcher? You bet. It's more than an interesting concept; it was reality every now and then in Double-X's career. Foxx came up to the Philadelphia Athletics as a catcher, and he caught some for the A's, when another catcher named Mickey Cochrane would let him. That much is preserved on his Diamond Star. You might not find a picture of Jimmie Foxx catching anywhere else, and even if you did, it wouldn't be rendered in such bright colors with so many bold geometric shapes in the background. That makes this card a nice piece of visual trivia. But that's not ample reason to go out and spend a couple hundred dollars to make this card yours. There are better reasons to do that.

Jimmie Foxx has languished in the shadows of Ruth and Gehrig ever since he retired and they died. But Foxx was every bit the equal of Ruth and Gehrig. Gehrig hit .340 for his career with 493 home runs. Foxx hit .325 for his career with 534 home runs. Foxx won three batting titles, four home-run titles and three runs-batted-in titles, without the supporting casts Ruth and Gehrig enjoyed. He was one of the game's greatest stars.

But Jimmie Foxx languishes, and he languishes most of all on baseball cards. Foxx appeared in only a handful of sets—the Goudeys, the Play Balls, and the Diamond Stars—and the Diamond Star Foxx is the best-looking, most undervalued of the bunch. Foxx ought to be the key card in the whole Diamond Stars set. He was the best player and biggest star in the set when it was issued, but he's far from being the most valuable card in the set today.

Some of the reasons for that have to do with the makeup of the Diamond Stars set. The cards were issued over a three-year period, and changes in the cards were made right along each year when they were necessary. The cards read, "One of 240 major-league players with playing tips," but the set is considered complete at 108 cards. Only 96 different players are shown, and 12 players from the 1934 series were repeated in the 1936 series. However, if you figure in all the front and back variations and combinations, the set contains 170 cards. The set's confusing to collect—most complete sets are technically incomplete—and that's hurt the set's popularity with collectors.

Though it includes practically every other Hall of Famer of the day, the set doesn't include Ruth or Gehrig. That hurts too.

The cards are also tough to find in top grades. While Diamond Stars were printed on heavy stock that has withstood the years well, the heavy cardboard tends to separate and soften at the corners, and take on a dirty, weatherbeaten appearance. Diamond Stars with solid corners and a pure white border are a real challenge to track down.

A Diamond Star Jimmie Foxx catalogs at $110. It cataloged at $85 two years ago. It's not headed anywhere special in a big hurry—maybe. But just maybe people will come around to how attractive these cards are, and how inexpensive they are, and how scarce they are in high grades. It's happened to virtually every set around the Diamond Stars, and it will happen to the Diamond Stars soon enough. Jimmie Foxx a catcher? You bet! What are you waiting for?

Paul's Score: 33

Kit's Score: 40

TOTAL SCORE: 73

1975 Topps
Robin Yount

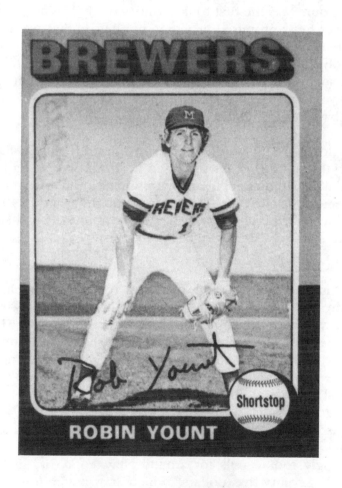

19

As you may have noticed by our flat accents and heavy shoes, your authors are from Wisconsin. We root for the Brewers and the Packers and Badgers and Bucks because if we don't we have our skin made into lampshades. The travel-and-tourism slogan for Wisconsin is, "You're among friends," but if you root for the Yankees you don't count.

Because we root for the Brewers and have for many years, we've watched the progress of Robin Yount from hatchling to superstar. Yount was the first rookie who actually was as good as the Brewer brass promised us would be. Before that we had to be content with promises that Ronnie "The Little General" Theobald would pick up where Pee Wee Reese left off. And he did, sort of. Reese hit .244 his last year. Theobald hit .276 his first year, and .220 his second, and after that there was no more pro baseball for Ronnie Theobald.

But Robin Yount was another story entirely. Robin has been everything the Brewers promised he would be, and a little bit more. They didn't necessarily promise us a Hall of Famer, but it appears we have one. With his 2,500 hits and .290 career batting average, his Most Valuable Player awards and string of great seasons, Yount looks like he has a spot reserved at Cooperstown.

The usual line of thinking once you reach that conclusion is, "Okay, the guy's a Hall of Famer. Let's go buy his rookie card." Then you go to buy Yount's rookie card and find it's $100 and rising by the day. Considering you've just come in from 1972, where you bought a Fisk-Cooper rookie for $12, and 1973, where you bought a Dwight Evans rookie card for $30, $100 may strike you as a bit steep.

It is expensive; no doubt about it. One hundred dollars is a lot to spend for a rookie card. But $85, which is what a Don Mattingly rookie sells for around New York City, is a lot to spend. Seventy-five dollars, which is what a Jose Canseco rookie can cost, is a lot to spend. But considering that Canseco and Mattingly are a long way from 2,500 hits and better than 100 triples and 187 home runs, and considering that Canseco and Mattingly rookies are as common as crabgrass, is $100 for a Yount rookie really that expensive? Sometimes perspective gets a little misplaced with rookie cards, and in the cases of Yount and his running mate in the 1975 set, George Brett, it gets lost altogether.

Forget for just a second the X's and O's of Yount rookies, and perspective and all that, and take a look at his rookie card. What a marvelously eager piece of work it is. There's nothing like the face of a 19-year-old when he's posing for his first major-league baseball card. Awe and wonder and a touch of cockiness and a little bit of fear and a whole bunch of natural ability; it all comes shining through in one simple little picture on cardboard. Robin Yount rookie cards are the reason people collect baseball cards. And that's not the Brewer fans in us speaking, either.

Paul's Score: 36

Kit's Score: 37

TOTAL SCORE: 73

1954 Topps
Ted Williams #250

20

ome of the best moments in baseball cards are those that defy logic the most. For instance, in the 1954 Topps set Ted Williams is card #1. He's also card #250. The cards are the same, or nearly so. Either one could be his regular card, but neither one is. Or maybe they both are. It just doesn't make any sense at all.

On second thought, it makes quite a bit of sense. Williams had never before been on a Topps card. He had been on a Bowman card in 1954, but was pulled to make room for Jimmy Piersall— at least, that's how Jimmy tells it. If Bowman had him but couldn't hold him, and Topps had never had him before, and Ted Williams being Ted Williams, greatest hitter in baseball and back from the service and all, why not put him on two baseball cards in the same set?

See? Perfect logic.

Of course, none of this explains why Williams was in the '55 Topps set but not the '56. Or why he was in the '57 and '58 sets but not the '59–'61. Those are stories for another time.

But back to the '54s. There's something funny about the Williams cards when you look at them closer. Williams is both the first and last cards in the set, and both cards carry the same price tag ($650 in Near Mint). Williams would absorb the abuse that comes with being the first or second card in three or more sets, making any high-grade Ted Williams card from the 1950s a tough card to find, but not as impossible as you might first think. A large percentage of #1 Williams cards are beat-up. But since first-series cards are almost always the most common cards in any given set, there are an awful lot of #1 Williams cards.

Williams would never again be the last card in the set, but last cards from high-number series are usually far tougher to find. Just based on that, you'd have to say the #250 Williams should be worth more than the '54 Topps #1 Williams.

Ha! Fooled you! The high-number series in the 1954 Topps set is actually as easy to find as the low-number series, according to the catalog. So if the #1 Williams is a $650 card, the #250 Williams ought to be a $650 card.

But wait again. Go to a show. Count up the #1 Williams cards you see and compare that to the number of #250 Williams you see. Which one do you see more? Maybe it's because we don't have Williams' 20/10 jet-pilot vision, but we see about twice as many #1 Williams cards as #250 Williams cards.

As we said, it defies logic. Baseball cards can be like that. That's one of the things we like best about them.

Paul's Score: 35

Kit's Score: 37

TOTAL SCORE: 72

1951 Bowman
Willie Mays

21

There's an ugly little undercurrent running through the baseball-card market that we might as well swim right into.

Though Jackie Robinson broke baseball's color line better than 40 years ago, there's still a subtle color line in the baseball-card market. Cards of black players are worth less than cards of white players of similar or lesser ability. And nowhere is that more evident than in the early cards of Mantle and Mays.

Mantle and Mays were and are and always will be *the* symbols of baseball in the 1950s. Mays flying flat-out, back to everything, chasing down Vic Wertz's drive like David Janssen going after the one-armed man, and getting it, cradling it with one last lunge at the very last moment. Mantle and that sweet, sweet, sweet all-or-nothing swing, launching America's first satellites and just watching them fly. That's all the near-poetry for this volume, we guarantee you, but Mantle and Mays were just so equal in everything they did on the field that it's dismaying to see such a gap between their cards.

And the gap is getting worse. Back in February 1988 Mantle's '51 Bowman cataloged at $2,000 in Near Mint. Mays' '51 Bowman—also his rookie card—cataloged at $750, or 37.5 percent of the Mantle. In July 1989 the Mantle cataloged at $4,800 while the Mays cataloged at $1,400, or 29.2 percent of the Mantle. Aesthetically they're similar cards, small and pretty and hard to find in high grades, and their historical significance is virtually identical. So why the disparity? Mantle is a more personable show guest than Mays, who gets a horrible case of the crotcheties any time he's brought within 20 yards of a Sharpie. That might have something to do with it. But the big reason is racial, and that's unfortunate.

The investor looking at a '51 Bowman Mays and comparing it to a '52 Mantle has to look at it this way: Solely on the basis of numbers the Mays is undervalued in comparison to the Mantle. But the baseball-card market doesn't always work solely on numbers. The baseball-card market sometimes works on prejudice. A reasonable person would think the prejudice can't last. That would be an improper assumption. Reason may triumph in the Mantle-Mays situation. But don't expect it to triumph anytime soon. The '51 Bowman Mays is a marvelously significant card with very little downside risk. It's just not what it could be.

• 1951 Bowman Willie Mays •

Paul's Score: 33

Kit's Score: 39

TOTAL SCORE: 72

T214 Mike Donlin

22

ome people, when they look at baseball cards, look at them as nothing much more than a place to put their money. And when some people look at places to put their money, they prefer Belgian-endive plantations and red-snapper farms to government-insured securities. It's the Belgian-endive people of the baseball-card market who'd appreciate the T214 Mike Donlin.

The player is suitably obscure, but good. Mike Donlin played 12 years, and hit an average of .333 for those years. The worst he hit in any one year was .294. He hit with power for the dead-ball era. Donlin has one of the highest batting averages of any veteran player not in the Hall of Fame. He fits in with Bill Dahlen and Vic Willis and some other near-Hall of Famers whose cards are meant for the prewar Cooperstown gambler.

The set is suitably obscure, too. The T214 set is probably the scarcest overall tobacco issue, and one of the scarcest of all card issues. The cards were given away only in Louisiana and only with Victory cigarettes. The Coupon and Red Cross issues are also Louisiana-only, but the Victory cards are rarer. In fact, they're so rare that only 30 cards of a set that's supposed to contain 90 cards have ever been found, and the other 60 will probably never be found. When a single T214 is found the entire obscure-tobacco-card segment of the hobby—such as it is—stops dead in its tracks. Long-time dealer David Festberg can remember having four or five of the cards in his life. One collector supposedly has eight or nine of the 30, and that's an enormous achievement. No one else is close.

The rarity of the T214s is their attraction, but when you're looking at the cards with an eye towards investing, it's also their biggest flaw. The cards are simply too rare to support any sort of demand for them. There's no way to make a market in T214s, because with a known universe of fewer than 500 cards there's no market.

The good news there is that as long as there are serious tobacco-card collectors there will be a ready, although quite limited, market for T214s. That may translate into modest profits, or that may translate into something more. It should translate into prices well above current catalog values ($200 in Donlin's case) if you're able to find one of those serious collectors. And he'll probably be grateful to you for selling if you do find him, too. You see it's hard to imagine anyone selling something so unusual—like a Belgian-endive farm.

Paul's Score: 38

Kit's Score: 34

TOTAL SCORE: 72

1933 Goudey
Hack Wilson

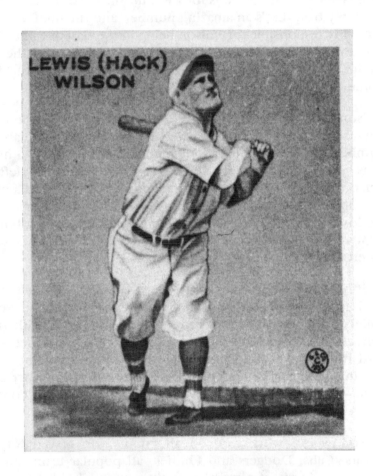

23

The best line ever uttered about Lewis "Hack" Wilson was that he was "a lowball hitter and a highball drinker." It was also the worst line ever written about Hack Wilson, for the highball drinking eventually caught up with the lowball hitting and drove him out of baseball prematurely.

Hack Wilson looked like an oil tank with legs and hit like nothing on earth. He made Kirby Puckett look like Kareem Abdul-Jabbar. But could he hit, and drive in runs, and hit home runs. He drove in 190 runs for the Cubs in 1930. Lively ball or no lively ball, that's an amazing number, and the number that's probably responsible for Wilson being in the Hall of Fame. That and the 159 runs he drove in the year before, and the five straight years of driving in 100 or more runs, and the four home-run crowns.

Wilson had short career for a Hall of Famer (12 years) and outside of the astounding season RBI and home-run totals, his numbers are sort of mundane: 1,461 hits, 1,062 RBI, 244 home runs. But Hack Wilson, like Lefty Gomez, was a definite personality, with his 16-inch neck and size-six feet and a chest that looked like he'd just swallowed one of those charcoal-mellowing vats of Jack Daniels. He helped make baseball in the 1930s the grand entertainment that it was, so he deserves to be where he is.

As it becomes increasingly difficult and expensive to get every card from every year, especially the early cards and years, collector/investors have to show a little ingenuity with their collection/portfolios. One option is to assemble a type set—one card from every set. It's expensive, and interesting, and not a bad investment if you choose your cards wisely. Another is by team—all the players who ever played for a team. A third option is to collect Hall of Famers.

Wilson would work well on all counts. He played for the Giants, Cubs, Dodgers and Phillies, all popular teams among collectors. Cards of players from those teams hold their value extremely well. As a second-division Hall of Famer, Wilson presents a good combination of availability, appreciation and value. You can find his card, buy it for a reasonable price, hold it for as long as you like, and sell it at a profit. And the '33 Goudey is the Wilson card of choice.

Unfortunately, a lot of people out there are thinking like you vis-a-vis the '33 Goudey Hack Wilson. The set's popular to start with, and for some reason the Hack Wilson card is one of the set's hottest cards. Near Mint examples of the card—and they're out there—sell for two or three times catalog ($55, last catalog).

John Brigandi advertised one in 1988. "I got about 17 calls on that card," he says now, and since he advertised that one card a few more cards in that grade have shown up in advertisements, but nowhere near the 17 needed just to keep up with demand. With more collectors entering the hobby every day, and with a '33 Goudey Wilson bound to be on somebody's want list, supply will likely continue to lag behind demand until prices increase to a point where they drive out more cards. That makes a '33 Goudey Wilson hard to find but worth finding.

Wilson may not have been too pretty in real life, but his card's a pretty thing indeed.

Paul's Score: 38

Kit's Score: 34

TOTAL SCORE: 72

1938 Goudey
Bob Feller

24

There are cards you buy for the beauty, knowing that someone somewhere will want to buy them for the beauty, too, and in the meantime you'll just get your enjoyment out of them. Then there are cards you buy for the investment potential, knowing that somewhere someone wants that card you have just to have it, and so you keep it until you know that other fellow just can't wait another second to have it, and you sell it to him and enjoy that. Then there are those cards you buy and hold onto and get out and look at again and look at one more time because they're just so darn homely you can't figure out if the company that made them actually thought kids would buy these up, or whether someone was just crazy or drunk or both. That's where the 1938 Goudey Bob Feller goes.

The set just doesn't make any sense. It consists of 48 cards, which is small enough, but 24 of the cards show the same players that are on the other 24! Each card appears twice, and the only difference from one appearance to the next is that the first time around the players are shown against a perfectly plain background, and the next time through the background is full of little cartoons and phrases.

Take an example. Card #264—for some reason, probably because the 1933 Goudey set left off at card #240, the '38 Goudeys are numbered starting with #240—shows Bob Feller. It shows a picture of Bob Feller's head plastered on top of a body about eight sizes too small. If Feller's body on this card were a shoe, Feller would get his toes in, and not much else. The '38 Goudey Feller #264 catalogs at $300.

Card #288 also shows Bob Feller. Same basic card, same eight-sizes-too-small body, only this time the background is filled with little cartoons and phrases. It catalogs at $350.

"Filled with little cartoons and phrases" isn't the way you want to go around describing a card's best attributes. And when the little cartoons and phrases are as corny-as-Kansas-in-August corny as these, it's no praise whatsoever. In the lower right corner of the Feller card you can feast on a boxcar-quality artist's rendition of corn stalks and clouds while reading that "Young Feller Hails From The Tall Corn Country." Deep. Profound. Profound even for baseball cards.

Oh, sure, there's been some bad art on baseball cards over the years. Horrible art. You'll never see the worst stuff, the stuff the authors see every day. The art has to be at least pretty good for the card to make it in this book. Even the strip cards have acceptable art. But the '38 Goudey Heads Up set is bad baseball-card art. Real bad baseball-card art. Baseball-card art so bad it's good.

That's right: so bad it's good. A major set don't come any worse than the '38 Goudey set, so everyone has to have one. The '38 Goudeys are the card equivalent of *The Rocky Horror Picture Show*: cult-classic cards.

What makes this set even classier—forget about the cult for just a second—is that it's historically significant. The set includes the first real cards of Bob Feller and Joe DiMaggio, two of each. And while they're bad cards, *Rocky Horror* cards, they are very important cards.

Valuable cards, too. There's a definite market for '38 Goudeys; no condition-rarity shallow-market business here. The plain Feller is up $100 in a year, and the doodled Feller is up the same amount over the same time. The doodled Feller gets the nod because it's the last card in the set and a condition rarity, and because it's so darn strange.

The '38 Goudey Feller is one wild card. And they can all be wild, if they all do as well as this card.

Paul's Score: 37

Kit's Score: 34

TOTAL SCORE: 71

1953 Bowman
Bauer, Berra, Mantle

25

ne of the crazy things about the baseball-card hobby is that more is usually less. For instance, a card company acts like it believes if it puts two or three big-name players on a baseball card that card ought to be two or three times more desirable than a card with any single big-name player on it. Au contraire, Eau Claire. It's the other way around. The more players on a card, big-name or not, the *less* it's worth. Sometimes it makes sense, sometimes it doesn't. This is one case where it doesn't make sense.

Yogi Berra is a Hall of Famer. Micky Mantle is a Hall of Famer, and hero for a generation of sandlot softball kids. Hank Bauer is . . . well, Hank Bauer, which is preferable to being Hud Podbelian. The three players are on a '53 Bowman color card, one of the most attractive cards ever made. Yet the card costs less than the single cards of Duke Snider or Whitey Ford, and far less than the single cards of Berra and Mantle.

Why? Not the aesthetics, certainly. It's a function of demand. Pay attention to this, because it'll show up later: *Demand is always greatest for a player's primary card. Any other card has to wait in line.* This holds for multiplayer cards, all-star cards, league-leader cards, turn-back-the-clock cards, career-retrospective cards, you name it. A collector with limited money to spend and a taste for high-grade specimens is much more likely to go after Berra's regular card, or Mantle's, or even the cards of Roy Campanella or Stan Musial, before buying the Mantle-Berra-Bauer card, nice as it is.

That's what happens in the real world. But the card company's original argument—if it has three times as many players on it, it must be three times as desirable—has some merit, too. You can get three for the price of one with this card, and it's certain to go up in value as the supply-demand curve continues to shift in the direction of demand with the 1953 Bowman set. And, heck, it's a gorgeous card. Bowman doesn't try to contrive any piece of business to explain the players being together, either, as Topps would do incessantly throughout the 1950s and 1960s. It's simply a card of three teammates being teammates. Its simplicity is its best selling point, and its beauty is undeniable.

•   1953 Bowman Bauer, Berra, Mantle   •

Paul's Score: 30

Kit's Score: 40

TOTAL SCORE: 70

T213
Walter Johnson

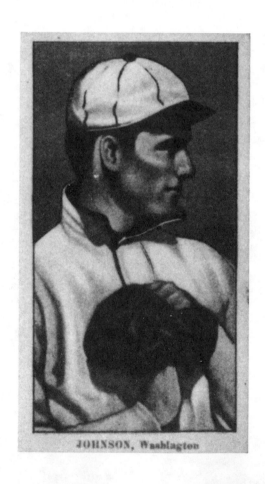

JOHNSON, Washington

26

What looks like a T206, is scarcer than a T206, tougher to find in nice shape than a T206, yet is often priced less than a T206? A T213 Coupon cigarette card.

All of the T213s were included in packages of Coupon cigarettes, which was a popular brand wherever it was sold. Unfortunately, it was only sold in Louisiana and a little bit of the surrounding area. Because of the Southern heritage of these cards, Southern League players are included in the set along with Federal Leaguers, American Leaguers and National Leaguers.

There are three different types of T213s. The first has a Coupon Mild advertisement on the back, and is printed on very thin stock, which makes it extremely tough to find in top grades. The second has a "20 for 5 cents" slogan on the back. These are printed on thicker stock but have a thick glossy coating that cracks and blemishes and makes it very hard to find in top grades.

Both these types of T213 include trades made after the T206s were issued. The cards also have some interesting mistakes, like listing Eddie Collins with the White Sox but picturing him with a big "A," for Athletics, on his uniform. In fact, three type II Collins cards are known: one shows him with Philadelphia, one lists him with Chicago but shows him in a Philadelphia uniform, and one lists and shows him with Chicago. It wasn't at all unusual for tobacco-card makers to update things as they went along, just like that.

The third type of T213s were printed on thicker stock, making them more durable than either of the first two types. They're also slightly smaller than the first two types, and advertise "16 for 10 cents" on the back. Sixty-nine different Type IIIs are known; commons are $40, and the whole set goes for around $4,300.

If T213s sound like everything you ever wanted in a tobacco card, listen again. The cards aren't well-known enough to be collectible, and they are not found in large enough quantities to make a market. No one really knows how many T213s of each type exist, and until a grading service or something similar can come along with a population report, we're not going to know. Until then, we just have to look on a Walter Johnson card like this and consider it a bargain, and buy it when we can find it. We're probably right, and we don't know when we might get another chance.

Paul's Score: 33

Kit's Score: 36

TOTAL SCORE: 69

T222 Fatima
Grover Cleveland
Alexander

Alexander–Phila. Nationals

27

carce. So many early cards are scarce, or rare or hard to find or seldom-seen, that you'd think scarce is the first name of most of these sets. Well, the fact is that just about all tobacco cards are scarce in top grades, and when you think about the chances of a piece of paper surviving 75 or 80 years and looking like the day it was first issued, it's a miracle any of them survive in any grade at all.

You can include the T222s in there. In 1914 Liggett and Myers produced the T222s, which were included in packs of its Fatima brand of cigarettes. At best, the set was uneven. Some clubs don't have a single player represented, while others have everyone but their mascot on a card.

The set features plenty of obscure players with short careers and is missing some of the big names of the day, including Cobb, Mathewson and Honus Wagner.

The set is scarce, and just about impossible to find in top collectible condition. The advertising pages of the hobby press are devoid of long listings of T222s for sale. If you're lucky, one shows up every few months.

Typically, amateur hobby historians know very little about the set. It was supposed to contain 100 subjects, but only 52 have turned up so far, although the rest could be the famous athletic champions and photoplay stars mentioned on the card backs.

The cards are printed on thin, bendable, creasable, brittle stock, which doesn't help the condition factor any. The black-and-white pictures further exacerbate the condition, so when you find a T222 it's likely to be covered with cobwebs of creases and imperfections. Looking for T222s without bends and creases is like looking for the Comstock Lode. You know it should be there, but you just can't find it.

If you do find it you should buy it, because it might be the last nice one you'll ever see. And if it happens to be one of Grover Cleveland Alexander, buy it without even thinking twice, because it ties in with the 1914 Cracker Jack Alexander as one of the first cards of one of the game's greats.

Alexander is a special challenge for card collectors because of his knack for missing out on most card sets. He started pitching in the majors in 1911, too late for the tobacco cards. He left in

1930, too early for the Goudeys. Alexander fell between the cracks and into that great cardless void of the 1920s (wonder if F. Scott Fitzgerald realized that). That leaves you to choose from among a Cracker Jack, some lesser issues and a T222. The Fatima is the choice, if you can only manage to find one.

Paul's Score: 34

Kit's Score: 35

TOTAL SCORE: 69

1986 Sportflics Canseco/Greenwell/ Tartabull Error

28

T
he hobby was abuzz in late 1985 because word was circulating that a fancy, high-tech set was going to be issued in 1986 by Wrigley Gum. Wrigley was going to teach Topps a thing or two, and maybe even put Donruss or Fleer out of the baseball-card business for good. That's the sort of thing that can get the hobby abuzz, and damn if the hobby didn't sound like a Yugo at full throttle.

Of course, the hobby was all abuzz in the wrong direction, though it was close. A fancy, high-tech major set was released in 1986, and Wrigley Gum was involved, but only a subsidiary of Wrigley Gum, and only as far away from the baseball-card end of things as it could get, in distribution. The subsidiary is Amurol, and they joined forces in 1986 with a printer of fancy, high-tech things called Optigraphics and some savvy baseball nuts called Major League Marketing to put out a set of cards called Sportflics.

Sportflics are an updated, tweaked version of the old Kellogg's wall-of-phlegm 3-D cards. The cards have the same heavy ribbed plastic coating on their front, but instead of having one prominent image pasted on a background of slime, Sportflics have three distinct images that change as the card is moved. It's done with prisms, they say, and it works. Tilt a card one way and you see a player portrait. Tilt it a little further and you see him starting his swing. Tilt it further still and you see him finishing his swing and breaking for first. Think of it as a very basic flip movie, or one one-millionth of an animated cartoon.

Think of it however you please, but also think of it as a gimmick. That's what collectors have done ever since the glow wore off the 1986 Sportflics set, and collectors hate gimmicks. Kids love gimmicks, though. Kids just absolutely love the heck out of gimmicks, and eat Sportflics whole. Sportflics are a tremendous retail product with no life whatsoever in the collector market. Sets sell to collectors at $28 and die two years later at $30. Even the collectors who claim to buy what they like don't seem to like Sportflics.

That's a shame. Sportflics deserve better from collectors. Maybe this is bourgeois baseball-card revisionism, but Sportflics have done a lot of good for the hobby. They gave Major League Marketing a chance to polish up its act for two years before going on to the "legitimate" Score set. They introduced to the hobby colorful, well-written, eyecatching card backs. They showed that a company or group of companies formed specifically to make and distribute baseball cards can pull it off successfully. And they proved that the cardmakers don't really need the hobby, much as the hobby might like to think otherwise.

Still, Sportflics shouldn't really be your set of first choice. While they may be seen as a good value someday, someday is a ways away. Also, the sets have never been good on rookies. The rookies that have shown up in Sportflics sets that haven't shown up in other sets have by and large been major fizzles. (Brick Smith? Mark Funderburk?) There is, however, one very major exception.

It's hard to figure out how everyone except Sportflics missed out on Mike Greenwell in 1986. Maybe everyone was so busy watching Jose Canseco and Herm Winningham and Jose Uribe that they forgot about Greenwell. But, hey, Greenwell hit .323 in a portion of a season in Boston, with four home runs and a couple more dingers off the Green Monster. In 1989 that would get him six rookie cards and most-favored-nation status. But 1986 was still something of a different time. People were conscious of big rookies, not every rookie. And Mike Greenwell, despite a .323 batting average, was Everyrookie.

That was good enough for Sportflics, though. Perhaps Sportflics was looking for an edge in its first year, and was shooting craps on rookies. Whatever the case, Greenwell landed on a rookie card with Superrookie Jose Canseco—it's also Canseco's rookie card, technically—Steve Lombardozzi, Mark Funderburk, Billy Joe Robidoux and Dan Tartabull. Each gets half of one of the three images that make up a Sportflics card. (Confused? You oughta be.)

For all that, the only Greenwell rookie and the Canseco rookie on the same card, it's only an $18 card. And that represents a big boost; at the start of 1989 it was a $6.50 card.

Six-fifty to $18. Oof. Does that mean more people are coming around to Sportflics cards? No. It means more people are coming around to this Sportflics card. And if you're only going to come around to one, this is certainly the one to come around to.

But wait. We're not finished. There's even more to this card. In the summer of 1989 a second version of this card was discovered. On the alternate version, Mark Funderburk's place is taken by an Indians first baseman Jim Wilson, who, as the card notes, broke his wrist late in the previous season and was hoping to make a comeback. Obviously he didn't, and Funderburk was substituted. The type size and style was changed on the back along with the copy.

This card is so rare nobody knows how rare it is. It's the equivalent of some of the great prewar rarities. Buy it now while there are still a few to be found relatively cheaply.

Paul's Score: 34

Kit's Score: 35

TOTAL SCORE: 69

1954 Topps
Ernie Banks

29

Baseball is a numbers game and a star game, but numbers and stars don't necessarily go hand in hand. Who do you consider to be the bigger star: Harmon Killebrew, Enos Slaughter, Johnny Mize, Eddie Mathews, or Ernie Banks? Banks normally gets the nod, though the others had comparable numbers.

Banks was a star and remains a star, on and off baseball cards, because of three factors: the team he played for, his performance and his demeanor. Willie Mays played for a New York team, posted tremendous numbers and was renowned for his on-the-field exuberance, but since his retirement he's been about as cordial as a rusty nail. He's still a baseball-card star, but not the star he could be. Mickey Mantle played for a New York team, posted tremendous numbers and was renowned for his aw-shucks Oklahoma demeanor, and he's kept it up after his retirement. He remains the game's premier baseball-card star.

But Banks is not far behind. He played for a team, the Chicago Cubs, that television made legendary around about the late 1960s, as Banks' career was easing into its twilight. Ever since 1969 there's been something magical, stupid and jug-eared and magical, about the Cubs. Banks and his "let's play two!" philosophy are a big part of that magic. Banks' performance is certainly Hall of Fame caliber, but middle-of-the-road Hall of Fame caliber. But Banks' demeanor on and off the field has always been delightful, personable and even-tempered. People, and that includes baseball-card collectors, like Ernie Banks. That explains why Banks' rookie card is $600.

Sorta. Al Kaline also has his rookie card in the same set, and it's a $575 card. But if you ask people outside of Detroit and Chicago (both cities get a wee huge bit xenophobic when the topic is their team) who was the bigger star, Banks or Kaline, the answer is bound to come up Banks most of the time.

If that's the case, something's rotten in the '54 Topps set. It's probably Al Kaline. It's hard to justify $575 for his card. But if his card is going to stay at $575—and it will—then the Banks card should be, say, $650 or $700. That would put it between Kaline and the other sort-of significant rookie in the set, Hank Aaron. And if that's going to happen, you ought to have a 1954 Topps Ernie Banks.

Ernie Banks is one of the few baseball stars who can still make you feel good about baseball. That means his card will always be in demand among collectors. That's nice. But it's not the point. Not really.

Paul's Score: 30

Kit's Score: 38

TOTAL SCORE: 68

1968 Topps
Bird Belters

bout 10 pages and six cards ago, we remarked that no matter how swell a card with more than one player on it looks, that card is still going to be worth less than the sum of the values of the cards of the separate players, and probably worth less than the cards of the separate players taken separately. It was true in 1953 Bowmans, it's true in 1964 Topps, and it's no less true in 1989 Fleers.

That's just the way it is. The more things change, the more people want the corrected versions.

Sometimes with multiplayer cards the injustice and the arithmetic match. For instance, is it such a crime that the Bill's Got It card, which features Bill Virdon and Danny Murtaugh, is only a 90-cent card? Is there any reason why the Angel Backstops card of Ed Sadowski and Bob Rodgers should exist, much less why it should cost more than 70 cents? And collectors can be forgiven if they consider a card that brings together at last Vada Pinson and Dick Sisler a less than essential item in their collections. These are the cards that give multiplayer cards a bad name. The name is "worthless."

It's a bad rap, to an extent. There are a few multiplayer cards in among the Pinson-Sislers and Sadowski-Rodgers that cost some money and are worth it. They show Hall of Famers in combination with other Hall of Famers or near Hall of Famers; they're delightful, and they're not bad buys, either.

The Casey Teaches Ed card in the '64 set shows Casey Stengel in an obviously staged shot offering some pointers to Ed Kranepool. It's a silly little card, but it has some character to it, and it's only $3. Multiplayer special card or not, that's the cheapest Casey Stengel card you're going to find by a long shot. The Sox Sockers card with Carl Yastrzemski and Chuck Schilling (five years, 23 homers, .239 lifetime) is $7, and is a similarly cheap Yaz card. All-Star Vets serves up the attractive combination of Nellie Fox and Harmon Killebrew for a dirt-cheap $4.

The golden age of multiplayer cards ran from about 1961 to 1969. One of the last great multiplayer cards appeared in the 1968 set; appropriately titled "Bird Belters", it shows Hall of Famers Frank Robinson and Brooks Robinson.

For all the captivation the Robinson boys laid on the American public in the 1960s, this is the only card that shows the two of them together. It's colorful, a high number, just a little hard to find perfectly centered, and is valued at $7 in Near Mint. That seems perfectly reasonable, considering that Brooks has a $12 card and Frank has a $10 card in the '69 set. If you want a '68 of both players and don't have $22 to lay down for the pair, this is an attractive alternative.

It will go up in value, too. The Bird Belters card has increased from $3 to $7 in the last two-plus years while the cards have moved from $16 to $22. You don't have to be much of a math whiz to realize that percentagewise the multiplayer card has the edge. And it will continue to be that way as long as the regular Robby cards experience price resistance and some collectors move down to the combo card.

As mentioned about six cards and 10 pages ago, multiplayer cards will never be worth the big bucks of the regular-run cards of the same playes. Is that important? Nah.

Paul's Score: 39

Kit's Score: 29

TOTAL SCORE: 68

1979 Topps
Ozzie Smith

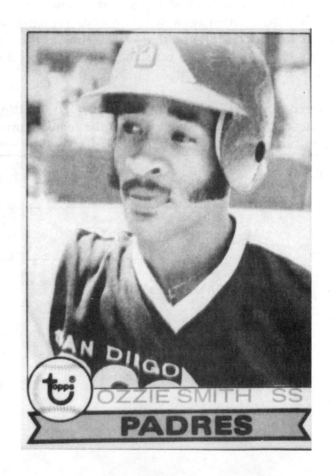

31

Do the rookie cards ever end? Nope.

Kit Kiefer gets some strange mail at *Baseball Cards* magazine. Some of it is of the "please send me all of Darryl Strawberry's cards so I can sell them and make money" variety, and does not get printed.

But a surprising amount of it reads, "Ozzie Smith is my favorite ballplayer, and I want to know why his rookie card isn't worth more." Well, the obvious answer is that Ozzie Smith's rookie card isn't worth more because Ozzie Smith doesn't hit home runs and drive in runs, or even hit for a high batting average that often, but that's not the right answer. It might explain why Jim Walewander's cards aren't worth more, but not Ozzie Smith's. Ozzie Smith is going to get into the Hall of Fame just the way Luis Aparicio did, and Rabbit Maranville did before him—on his glove—and many segments of the hobby just can't realize that. And they're going to be left by the wayside.

Ozzie's an okay hitter—his career average is .255—and he can steal bases with the best of them—better than Aparicio, actually—but what Ozzie Smith has brought to the game is acrobatics. The diving catch, the leaping snare, the accurate throw, the back flip: these are the things that people remember about Ozzie Smith, and will continue to remember long after Smith has retired, and that will eventually earn Smith a spot in the Hall of Fame. Smith has redefined the way shortstop is played, and the Hall of Fame people look very kindly on that.

His card doesn't exactly reflect Smith's contributions to the game. It's $20, a modest $20. Only recently has it moved up to that level. People are paying a little more attention to Ozzie Smith's rookie card these days, which suggests it's time to buy. Smith has already made his mark on the game. He could probably hit .190 for another two years and quit, and his place in Cooperstown would be safe. He's simply been too good at what he does for too long for his reputation to fade away or his card to drop in value.

This is one of those sure-thing rookie cards. It's safe. And as the kids who keep the cards and letters coming continue to point out, it's going to be safe for a long time.

Paul's Score: 32

Kit's Score: 36

TOTAL SCORE: 68

1952 Topps
Bill Dickey

32

Take another look at those rankings of high-number Hall of Famers with Willie Mays. In your opinion, which one of those cards is the most undervalued? If you're a contrarian, you'll be contrary and say Mantle. If you're a Cub fan then you're already contrary, so you say Billy Herman. If you're over 50 and cut your fingernails you say Hoyt Wilhelm. If you can't see your shoes you say Early Wynn. If you're a citrus fruit you say Bob Lemon. But if you're shrewd you say Bill Dickey.

Dickey is a Hall of Fame catcher, and with Mickey Cochrane arguably the best catcher ever. He played for 17 years with the Yankees, hit. 313, played on eight World Series teams, and taught and led and played the game square. No catcher has been able to combine offense and defense as long or as successfully as Dickey, and though his longevity records have been broken, Dickey remains the greatest Yankee catcher of all time. Considering his competition includes Yogi Berra, Elston Howard and Thurman Munson, that says something.

Why then has Dickey's card only budged $50 in the last two years? The Monty Python factor: He's not dead yet. Also, the '52 Topps card in question shows Bill Dickey as a coach, not a catcher. The hobby has limited contact and experience with coaches' cards, especially high-number '52 Topps cards of Hall of Famer coaches. The temptation is to transpose eras, forget how good Dickey was, price his card at a level less than managers and much less than active players and then freak out, or maybe skip the first three steps and just freak out. Billy Herman falls into the same category, with a thud.

If you're going to buy a '52 Topps Dickey, hold out for top quality. That's always a good idea, but with Dickey it's a better idea because high-grade cards will be in greater demand after Dickey's death, and because current values for high-grade Dickey cards don't reflect how scarce they really are. Dickey is card #400, seven cards from the end of the set. Card #407, Ed Mathews, is the end card and an $1,800 card in top grade. That price is so high because kids are kids, and they supposedly keep their cards rubber-banded together in numerical order and bang up the first and last cards in the stack. Fair enough, but the $1,800 value for the Mathews card presumes he was always the last card in the stack. Dickey's card is as likely to have been the last card in the stack, at least for a time, and to have absorbed plenty of abuse. Next time you go to a show, see how many mid-grade '52 Topps Dickeys with rubber-band notches you can find. It's not hard. Then see how many clean, sharp examples you can find. If that doesn't separate you from $500 on the spot nothing will.

Paul's Score: 33

Kit's Score: 35

TOTAL SCORE: 68

1983 Topps
Wade Boggs

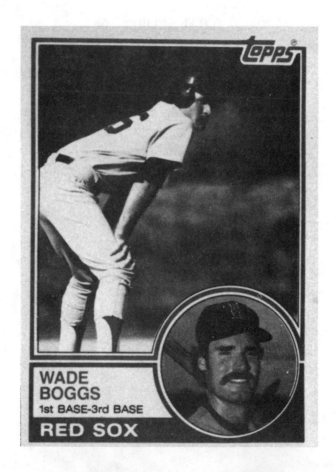

WADE
BOGGS
1st BASE-3rd BASE
RED SOX

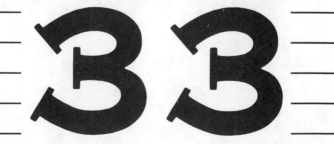

Wade Boggs' rookie card is the most expensive card in the 1983 set, and twice as expensive as the Tony Gwynn rookie. But expensive isn't necessarily valuable, and expensive doesn't necessarily make the card one of the top 100 baseball cards of all time. Wade Boggs makes the Wade Boggs rookie one of baseball's top 100 cards. His card is a relatively disposable thing.

Wade Boggs' card is valuable solely because of what Wade Boggs does for a fraction of his time on a baseball field. Boggs is perceived as the best scientific hitter of his day, and superior to Tony Gwynn because of it. Gwynn sees the ball and hits it; Boggs breaks the hitting process down to its neuromuscular components, studies the physiology of the swing, trains and disciplines eyes and brain and muscles and tendons and bones to deliver him a constantly flawless swing, and takes every bit of the fun out of the game in the process. There's no sense of joy, no sense of childhood recaptured, no sense of love for the game with Wade Boggs, just an unattractive grimness.

But Rogers Hornsby was grim and Ty Cobb was unattractive. The solitary fact that Boggs is such a great hitter—yes, a little better hitter than Tony Gwynn—*is* enough to justify the significance of his rookie card. The card stands for something, attractive or not, and it's only a bad buy in comparison to other cards in the 1983 set. Thirty-two dollars for the card of the best hitter in baseball, with Darryl Strawberry's rookie card in that year's Update set at $60? The price for the Boggs card seems fair; the price for the Strawberry card doesn't.

But keep a couple of things in mind before you cash in the insurance policies and go buy Wade Boggs cards. The card hasn't moved much in relation to Boggs' on-the-field performance. Two and a half years ago Wade Boggs had three batting titles and a $21 card. Now Wade Boggs has at least five batting titles and a $32 rookie card. Even at seven bucks to a batting title the modern Boggs comes up $3 short.

That could mean one of two things: Either Boggs' rookie card is honestly lagging behind Boggs' on-the-field performance, and is going to catch up one of these days, or no amount of batting titles is going to pump up his card, and every time he doesn't win a batting title his card's going to stand in mortal danger of dropping in value. Winning a batting title isn't like eating a Twinkie, you know; just because Boggs makes it look

that easy (though not any fun at all), he shouldn't be expected
to do it every year.

The Wade Boggs rookie card is a real paradox. It's overvalued
and undervalued at the same time, and simultaneously desirable
and undesirable, too. If you like it, buy it. But if you wonder
about it, you're not alone.

Paul's Score: 38

Kit's Score: 29

TOTAL SCORE: 67

1953 Bowman
Casey Stengel
(B&W)

34

The 1953 Bowman black-and-white series has always befuddled collectors. They've never quite been able to figure out why Bowman switched from a color series to a black-and-white series 161 cards into what would have been a 224-card set. Economics is the explanation usually offered, and it makes some sense—Bowman was a smaller and less financially secure company than Topps, and was always battling the high production costs of good-looking cards on one hand and Topps on the other—but bewilderment is probably just as good an explanation for what happened to Bowman in 1953. Bowman executives simply didn't have any idea how much these things would cost, and once they got the bills they realized they couldn't afford to do what they'd been doing, and they had to do something different. In the case of the 1953 Bowman set, it meant going to black and white.

And there is nothing wrong with black-and-white 1953 Bowmans. A lot of collectors treat them like pariahs, but they're not as common as 1953 color Bowmans, and much tougher to find in high grade. Some collectors shun the set because it doesn't have any good players, but that's just plain ignorant. The set has cards of four Hall of Famers plus early cards of Lew Burdette, Ralph Branca and Jimmy Piersall. The only thing wrong with the cards is they're not in color, and even though they are the best-looking black-and-white cards ever made, that's just not good enough.

Only one card in the '53 Bowman B&W series is worth more than $90, and that's the card of Casey Stengel. You couldn't find a more dramatic card anywhere in the '53 Bowman color set. Stengel was made to be photographed in black and white; the black sinks into the lines on the Yankee manager's face, and the shadows deepen and take on a disturbing starkness. This card takes the typical managerial pose—one foot on the dugout step peering out on the field—and turns it into a morality play, a metaphor for man's struggle against fate, a veiled lesson for the entire human race.

Well, maybe that's pushing it, but it is a handsome card. A pretty good buy, too. It's moved up about 60 percent in the last two years but it's still affordable. And because Casey Stengel cards show up so seldom in the sets of the 1950s and 1960s—only nine times on regular cards from 1950 and 1965—it's a significant card as well.

And now, the rest of the story. The rest of the story is about a set of big, beautiful Bowman cards. The cards had colorful fronts, and some of the most appealing pictures ever seen on cards. They're some of the best cards made, and today they bring big bucks because of that. But the cards are hard to find, only in part because of their beauty. The other part is that at some point in the press run Bowman realized it wasn't making money on the cards, and couldn't make money on the cards, and it stopped production. And when Bowman resumed production it made the *same* cards—only smaller! The year was 1952. The cards were football cards. Out of the packs Bowman could never get its act together. But the packs and the cards were a different story altogether.

Paul's Score: 29

Kit's Score: 38

TOTAL SCORE: 67

1963 Topps
Tony Oliva

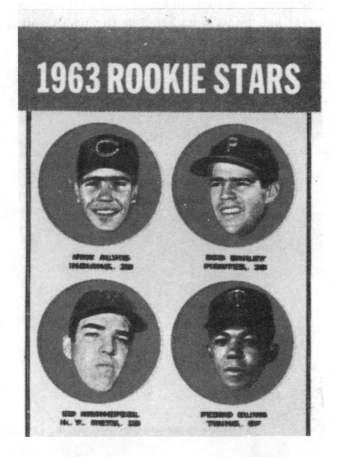

I n the 1963 Topps set, there's one great rookie card. It may be *the* premier rookie card of the 1960s; that's how good it is. People who know next to nothing about baseball cards know a little about this card. This story is not about that card.

That card is the 1963 Topps Rookie Stars card featuring Pedro Gonzalez, Ken McMullen, Al Weis, and a young Reds infielder named Pete Rose. It's a tremendously unattractive card and, at $600 and with Pete Rose's legacy in doubt, it's just not much of a buy.

The card that is more of a buy, and the card this story's about, is also a Rookie Stars card. But instead of showing Rose et al., this card shows Ed Kranepool, bonus-baby Bob Bailey, Max Alvis, and a young Twins outfielder named Tony Oliva.

Tony Oliva may not have a place at Cooperstown all wrapped up, but he has a much better shot than you might think. Oliva, when he was healthy—and even when he wasn't—was the dominant hitter in the American League in the 1960s and early 1970s. His batting titles and hit titles are some proof of that, but the real proof comes when you talk to American League pitchers of that era. To a man—*to a man,* from Bill Lee to Jim Bouton to Catfish Hunter—they all say the best hitter they ever faced was Tony Oliva. That's the sort of testimony that gets players into Cooperstown, through the Veterans' Committee if not through the sportswriters' balloting.

What makes this card attractive—and it's really no more of an aesthetic pleasure than the Pete Rose rookie—is that it's only $25. The Rusty Staub rookie in the same set is $25, and Oliva stands a better shot of making it into Cooperstown than the Orangeman. Even Bill Freehan's rookie card is $20 in this set. Oliva comes off looking like a bargain.

There has been some price movement lately on this card—from $9 to $25 in the last year and a half. It's almost as though collectors expect Oliva to be elected to the Hall of Fame. The collectors just might be right.

Paul's Score: 35

Kit's Score: 31

TOTAL SCORE: 66

1983 Fleer
Tony Gwynn

36

y 1983 Fleer had figured out what it wanted to do with its cards for the rest of its life. It cleaned up the errors, and bid adieu to the junk-can, telephoto-lens snapshots; Fleer told its photographers it wanted *photographs* from them, by God, and photographs they got, and have ever since. Then Fleer took the photographs and actually did something nice with them, cropped them short like a small-town barber would, and stuck them inside pleasant gray frames. The result was cool and classy, the best of the pre-boom sets, and even if Fleer did choose this set to perfect its terrifically soporific backs (no one must read card backs; that's all we can figure out), it's still a great-looking set that comes cheap.

The set has all the key cards of 1983—Gwynn, Boggs and Sandberg—and you can pick and choose which key cards you want from which set. Here the pick card is Tony Gwynn. Gwynn is to National League hitting what Boggs is to American League hitting, no more and very little less. Gwynn has three batting titles and a career .331 average. He has Boggs' occasional home-run power and averages about the same number of hits per year as Boggs. But Gwynn has better stolen-base speed—he co-holds the major-league record for most stolen bases in a game—and is a much better position player.

So why then, why is Boggs' card exactly twice as expensive as Tony Gwynn's—$18 as opposed to $9, in the Fleer set?

Boston.

Cards of New York Yankees, New York Mets, Boston Red Sox and Philadelphia Phillies are automatically 10 percent to 25 percent more expensive—expensive, mind you, not valuable—than cards of the other players from other teams. It gets a little silly sometimes, when a misguided rookie card of a Double-A Yankee shortstop sells for as much as the rookie card of that year's rookie of the year, but it's simple supply and demand. The Northeast has more collectors. They want the cards of their players, who are usually Yankees, Mets, Phillies, and Red Sox. When more people want a static number of cards the price goes up. You can make money off this—buy Yankee cards in North Dakota and sell them in New York—but it's an awfully mercenary way to make a living. You might be better off pursuing nobler aims, like Yankee-hating or Met-bashing. Or running semi-automatic weapons.

Wade Boggs' card is twice as expensive as Tony Gwynn's because Boggs plays in Boston and Gwynn doesn't, and because the perception is that Boggs is a much better hitter than Gwynn, and Gwynn has just been on a crazy streak of luck or something. That's unfair to Gwynn. His card has moved up only $3 in the last two years, basically because collectors don't appreciate the '83 sets, and allow them to pale in comparison to the '84 boom sets. That's unfair to Gwynn, too. With every batting title from now on, Gwynn's card will appreciate arithmetically or factorially or something like that. It will increase in value at an increasing rate; that's it. Appreciate that appreciation while you can.

Paul's Score: 36

Kit's Score: 30

TOTAL SCORE: 66

1984 Fleer Update
Dwight Gooden

37

One of the most wonderful things about 1984 was that things started out with Don Mattingly and just got better from there. Later in that year Fleer came out with its first Update set. It wasn't sure how many to make, and buyers weren't sure how many to buy. Then some things happened, and the roof blew off Fleer Update sets.

First and foremost, Dwight Gooden happened. Gooden was the pitching incarnation of Darryl Strawberry, a strikeout pitcher who pitches for the Mets, and he captured the public's fancy even more completely than Darryl. He tore off a great hunk of a rookie season—17 wins, 9 losses, a 2.60 earned-run average, a record-setting 276 strikeouts—and won the loop's rookie-of-the-year award.

People wanted Dwight Gooden's baseball card. But Dwight Gooden didn't have a baseball card—at least, not a major-league one. And Gooden didn't have a major-league baseball card until Topps and Fleer came out with their traded/update sets.

It's funny, but people didn't drive up the price of Fleer Update sets trying to get at Dwight Gooden cards right away. The Gooden thing was a little slow in building. But once it built, boy, it built itself up like a skyscraper. Fast, too. All through late 1984 and early 1985 more and more people tried to buy a static number of Dwight Gooden cards. The price went up, and so more and more people tried to buy a smaller static number of Gooden cards. It was the Mattingly scenario all over again, only with an even greater degree of perceived scarcity. By the end of 1985 Dwight Gooden's Fleer Update card was $90. In a little more than a year the card went from a dime to $90. It reinforced the message the Donruss Mattingly had delivered several months earlier: "Baseball cards can go up in value. Big time. You like baseball cards better than common stocks. You still might have that shoebox in your mother's attic. You should buy baseball cards." That message first delivered by the Mattingly and Gooden cards in 1984 is still being delivered in the same form today.

But the Gooden card also delivered another message: What goes up can come down, even in baseball cards. Personal problems (alleged alcohol and drug abuse) kept Gooden out of the majors for part of the 1987 season. His card lost half its value overnight. Met and Yankee cards weren't supposed to do that. They were supposed to be oblivious to downturns as long as the players on the cards remained Mets and Yankees. Gooden proved that theory wrong. His Fleer Update card was lapped by the first card of the new fireball ace, Roger Clemens, which is also in the '84 Fleer Update set, and eventually nosed out by the first card of the Twins' Plump Stump of Thump, Kirby Puckett. Even though the card has regained most of its lost value—it's up to $75 now—some buyers still expect an eventual relapse, and remain leery.

Some dealers will say the Fleer Update Gooden is still undervalued at that level. Other dealers will point out how many Carlton Fisk rookies or Dwight Evans rookies or Trammell-Molitor rookies you can buy for that $75. Some dealers will bring up scarcity. Other dealers will go out for coffee and a sweet roll. And if a Fleer Update Gooden sounds good to you, go right ahead. You won't be wrong.

Paul's Score: 27

Kit's Score: 38

TOTAL SCORE: 65

1941 Play Ball
Lefty Gomez

"LEFTY" GOMEZ

38

The 1941 Play Ball set is a favorite. Nobody doesn't like the 1941 Play Ball set. It has grand, desirable, colorful cards of Joe DiMaggio and Ted Williams, and a Pee Wee Reese rookie, and cards of Hall of Famers everywhere.

All of those cards could be among the 100 best of all time, for their looks and their appreciation potential and the aura around them. But they've been edged aside ever so slightly by a card of Vernon "Lefty" Gomez, the Hall of Fame pitcher with a blazer of a fastball, a love for airplanes and a truly screwy attitude.

Gomez may have been swallowed up some in his day, playing on teams whose marquee players were Ruth, Gehrig and DiMaggio. But don't overlook Gomez or his cards the way some collectors have. The lefthander's lifetime 189–102 record was pretty special, as was his record of six World Series victories in seven starts.

And as for that screwy attitude, it was Gomez who lit a match at home plate, not so he could better see Bob Feller's pitches, but so Feller could better see him. It was Gomez who would stop the game to watch an airplane pass overhead (a habit which would really slow down things in today's Shea Stadium, which lies directly in the flight path for LaGuardia airport), and Gomez who one day took a plane and buzzed the stadium. When his manager told him, "Boy, you should have been here yesterday. Some crackpot flier was diving and spinning all over the place," Gomez answered along the lines of "That was me. Not bad, huh?" Ol' Lefty will be missed.

Lefty was the product of a different era of baseball, and so is his '41 Play Ball card. The '41 Play Balls were the last cards made by the Philadelphia Gum Co. (the last *baseball* cards, until this past year), and the last major prewar set. World War II affected baseball cards more severely than it did baseball. While the prewar card industry wasn't an industry at all but an occasional offshoot of the bubblegum and candy industry (which was hardly an industry itself), at least baseball kept on playing through the war. Baseball cards ceased production altogether, and were among the last consumer products to resume production after the war. It was 1947 or '48 before any baseball cards of note reappeared on grocers' shelves.

Furthermore, many 1941 Play Balls were the first to go in wartime paper drives that also claimed untold numbers of

Goudeys, Diamond Stars and DeLongs. The fact that the Play Balls were some of the most beautiful cards ever produced, with their gently tinted artwork and stylized backgrounds, meant little at paper-drive time. When you think about the country's mood during the war years, with patriotism galloping around everywhere, it's a wonder that *any* prewar cards survived.

The 1941 Play Balls are printed on thin stock (making those high-grade cards that much more valuable), and can often be found in uncut sheets or strips. The cards from 49–72 are scarcer than the lower numbers; Reese is in that series, along with DiMaggio, Bill Dickey and Gomez.

In fact, Gomez is the last card in the set. Since '41 Play Balls are fragile to begin with, and since older cards were often kept rubber-banded in numerical order, the Gomez card shapes up as a condition rarity of the first degree. Chances are that if a card is going to get banged up out of the '41 Play Ball set, it'll be a Gomez. That makes the card a buy, and the current Near Mint value of $200 out of date—as out of date as the idea of a pitcher who stopped the game to watch an airplane fly by.

Paul's Score: 36

Kit's Score: 29

TOTAL SCORE: 65

1957 Topps
Brooks Robinson

ur pal the Constant Rater, a pro ballplayer of no repute who writes a regular feature for *Baseball Cards* magazine, says he's never been all that impressed by Brooks Robinson.

"Lookit, the guy's just a leatherhand," Constant said to us one day when we were all sitting around a can of Hi-C cutting down Hall of Famers. (Leatherhand is his term for a ballplayer that's all glove and not much bat.) "What's his batting average? Two-sixty? And how many home runs did he hit? Two-hundred-some? Not good enough. And that's with that Oriole dynasty of the 1960s, where he couldn't have had more fat served to him if he had ordered the chicken-fried-steak special at Millie and Tillie's Big Eat Cafe. Stan Hack hit .301 with no help from the Cubbies, *and* no fat *and* played a great third base, and is he anywhere near Cooperstown? Huh? And do you think they'll bow down for Buddy Bell, even though he had a higher batting average and nearly as many home runs and hits as Brooksie when he retired, *and* just as good a reputation as a fielder? The only reason George Kell was elected to the Hall of Fame was because the guys felt guilty for rushing in Brooksie the way they did. Hey, they didn't just elect Brooks Robinson to the Hall of Fame. They *canonized* the guy, and I don't mean nothin' that H&B does to a bat."

Well, perhaps the Constant Rater has a point, and it's not just the Hi-C talking for once. Then again, perhaps not. As a one-dimensional player himself—that dimension being popping up puffball 3–0 cripple fastballs—the Constant Rater appreciates players who can add to that one dimension the skills of grounding into double plays and starting in on balls hit over his head. Brooks Robinson was just never his kind of player.

Brooks Robinson redefined the way third base should be played. The acrobatic leap, the last-second dive, the reflex play: they had existed before, but never in a package like the one Brooks Robinson put together. All the great-fielding third basemen who came before Brooks had their accomplishments put into a new perspective by Brooks. All great-fielding third basemen who came after Brooks would have to be compared to Brooks, and would usually be found wanting.

If that's the case, what then to make of his rookie card, #328 in the 1957 set? It's a $300 card, expensive for a '57; only Ted Williams, Mickey Mantle and a Mantle-Berra special card are worth more. But it's in a high-number series where any common card is $15. Take out that high-number factor and the Brooks Robinson rookie card is actually less than the Frank Robinson rookie (which is as it should be, in all honesty). It's been moving up in price more slowly than other cards in the '57 set, but a glossy, well-centered example hasn't become any easier to find, and Robinson hasn't lost his title of best defensive third baseman of all time.

So maybe the card has some catching up to do. If it does, one thing's certain: if it involves catching, Brooks Robinson will make sure it gets caught, and stays caught.

Paul's Score: 28

Kit's Score: 37

TOTAL SCORE: 65

T204 T.T.T.
Ed Kargar

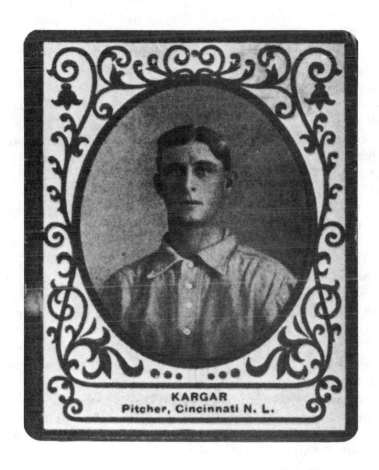

KARGAR
Pitcher, Cincinnati N. L.

40

While it is true that the career highlights of Ed "Loose" Kargar are just about equal to the season highlights of the '62 Mets, his T204 card is nice. Kargar won 15 games in 1907, though that was accomplished at the expense of losing 19, and after losing 19 the year before. Yes, Ed "Loose" Kargar was loose with the hits and runs. He'd better have a nice T204 card.

All T204s are nice, especially if you like the wallpaper in old hotels. T204s have black-and-white pictures inside these ornate, country-living borders that are either captivating or tacky, depending on your taste in rococo antimacassars and gilt geegaws. If you like the borders, you're faced with finding the cards, which is not easy, especially examples which carry advertisements for T.T.T. Turkish cigarettes on their backs. (The more common T204s advertise Ramly cigarettes.) You'll also have to put your love for the borders up against the fact that the set has only Walter Johnson, Wee Willie Keeler, Chief Bender, Eddie Collins, Ed Plank and Clark Griffith for big names. Ty Cobb, Christy Mathewson, Honus Wagner, and Tris Speaker are elsewhere. Maybe they couldn't stand the borders.

T.T.T.-back cards are only a small percentage of the total population of T204s, which isn't very large to start with. Even if the card is of Ed Kargar, it's a scarcity few people run across and a surprising number of people would pay a surprising amount above its catalog value ($125) to have it.

Like all early tobacco cards, the T204 T.T.T.-back Kargar is a solid card that will go up right along with the market, and might even beat the market by 50 percent or so in the short term, if you buy right and sell right. The T.T.T. back gives you a lot of extra scarcity for not much extra money. It's the way to go with T204s.

But if you can't stand the borders, forget we ever said anything.

Paul's Score: 33

Kit's Score: 32

TOTAL SCORE: 65

1959 Topps
George Anderson

41

N ow here's a card you ought to have. It's the card of a pretty good fielding infielder with a little bit of smarts who hit all of .218 in one season and one season only with the Philadelphia Phillies. Could be Ed Spezio, could be Bobby Ethridge. A sure candidate for the commons box, right? Try again. Try $12 for the rookie card of this light-hitting infielder. And you want to know something else? The card's underpriced at $12. That light-hitting infielder is a shoo-in for the Hall of Fame—not for what he did on the baseball diamond, but for what other players did under his guidance. You see, the infielder is named George Anderson, but the future Hall of Famer is named Sparky Anderson. They're one and the same, and the people who realize that realize what a bargain this card is.

Of course, the only way this card's a bargain is if Sparky Anderson really is a shoo-in for the Hall of Fame. Well, Sparky won better than 870 games, five division titles, two N.L. titles, and two World Series with Cincinnati, then took over the Tigers in 1979 and won another 820 games, two division titles and a World Series with them. His winning percentage is somewhere around .570, and considering anything above .550 is considered by the SABRmetricians to be a darn sight better than peanut butter and jelly, and considering that Hall of Fame manager Walter Alston (who sure didn't get into the Hall on the strength of *his* playing record) only has a winning percentage of .558, Sparky looks to be on pretty firm footing. The fact that he never met a microphone he didn't like shouldn't hurt his chances at all.

The Hall of Fame isn't the sort of place that welcomes in managers as if they were, say, Candy Cummings. Anderson will get some competition for his spot among baseball's immortals (like Morgan Bulkeley and the aforementioned Mr. Cummings) from Whitey Herzog. Anderson is probably the best manager in the American League, and Whitey is probably the best manager in the National League. Whitey won three straight division titles with the Royals and two N.L. flags and a World Series with the Cardinals, but Anderson has more wins and a better overall winning percentage. And Whitey looks like the guy down at the foundry who sticks out his beer gut and calls it Lucille, and beats on his chest with an aluminum baseball bat because it's his coffee break.

That may be, but Herzog's rookie card, in a common series in the 1957 Topps set, costs $18. When you put it on a constant-dollar basis with Sparky's rookie, Herzog's card is cheaper by a couple of bucks, but it ought to be. And Herzog's card has gone up farther faster than Anderson's, and that's not right, either. Anderson's card should cost more and go up faster, and right now it hasn't done either.

And look at it this way: You can't buy a 1950s rookie card of a Hall of Famer or a wanna-be Hall of Famer for less than $12, unless your idea of a wanna-be Hall of Famer is Jerry Lumpe. Even a guy like Orlando Cepeda, who has about eight ounces of marijuana standing like a 900-foot-tall wall between him and Cooperstown, has a $25 rookie card. Anderson doesn't have one of those walls; all he has is a cheap rookie card and a mouth that won't quit, and teams that just keep winning ballgames. That oughta suffice.

Paul's Score: 29

Kit's Score: 35

TOTAL SCORE: 64

1933 DeLong
Riggs Stephenson

42

T he 1933 Goudey set is famous for being the first major gum set, and rightfully so. But the 1933 DeLong gum set deserves a little bit of that spotlight too.

The DeLong Gum Co. of Boston packaged baseball cards with its product at the same time Goudey Gum packaged baseball cards with its product. But DeLong never could match Goudey's distribution and DeLong's cards were less attractive than Goudey's, so what turned into a profitable way of selling gum for Goudey turned into a one-shot deal for DeLong.

The DeLong set is long on Hall of Famers; more than half the players pictured in the set made it to Cooperstown. The cards elicit love-hate reactions; people who like having a real big black-and-white player picture superimposed over a real little stadium like the cards. People who don't, don't. Backs feature playing tips from the ubiquitous Austen Lake, editor of the *Boston Transcript* (and author of the backs for Diamond Stars).

The DeLong set comes up short artistically only in comparison to contemporary Goudeys and its hand-painted predecessors. The set comes up short otherwise only because it lacks Babe Ruth. Everyone else is there, except for some common players (Earl Adams et al.) included by Goudey but passed over by DeLong. And no one feels the set suffers much for missing out on that.

The current price relationship between Goudeys and DeLongs is a joke. High-grade DeLongs are at least twice as difficult to find as Goudeys, yet are only slightly more expensive than comparative Goudeys. If Goudeys are the next "hot" set of older cards, as many experts believe, then DeLongs ought to go right up with them—ahead of them, actually. Top-condition DeLongs already sell for two or three times their catalog values. Once the catalog values are readjusted to reflect that reality, the cycle can start in all over again. DeLongs are in the middle of an upward price spiral.

And if there is a sleeper in a set that's half Hall of Famers, it's Riggs Stephenson. Stephenson is the only player left in the set who still has a realistic shot at Cooperstown. Riggs Stephenson has one of the highest lifetime batting averages (.336) of any player with his number of at-bats (4,500) and hits (1,500) who is not in the Hall of Fame. Except for 74 at-bats in his last year in the majors, Stephenson never hit less than .296. Dead ball,

127

live ball, mud ball, it doesn't matter—that's hitting. Stephenson wasn't renowned for his glove, but neither was Hack Wilson. Stephenson's numbers compare favorably to those of Ross Youngs and Wilson (except for the home runs and runs batted in), and aren't too far removed from Kiki Cuyler's.

Stephenson is a sleeper card in an undervalued set that's in the midst of an upward price spiral. What more could you ask for?

Paul's Score: 32

Kit's Score: 32

TOTAL SCORE: 64

E102
Christy Mathewson

43

There ought to be more of a fuss made over the first gum cards. People ought to buy the first gum cards hand over hand just out of gratitude for everything chewing gum has done to their lives. Face it: if there hadn't been chewing gum, the gum companies wouldn't have felt the need to put baseball cards in their gum packs, because there wouldn't have been any gum packs because there wouldn't have been any gum. If there hadn't been baseball cards, there wouldn't be football cards or basketball cards or the $750 million-a-year baseball-card industry/market, or this book or the advance on this book or . . . we'd better just stop right there.

Over here is the E102 set. It's the Wise Buy black-and-white label generic candy-and-gum set. It has a little bit of the E92 set, and some of the pictures of the E101 set, and a little bit of the look of the E105 and T216 tobacco set. It's the sort of pirated candy set that gives candy sets a bad name.

What it also does to candy sets is make them relatively inexpensive in lower grades, and theoretically cheaper than comparable—very comparable—tobacco cards. It sets up a situation where early candy cards are to early tobacco cards what modern football cards are to modern baseball cards: a lower-priced alternative to higher-priced cards. If modern football cards only showed modern baseball players on them it would be perfect.

But old candy cards do have pictures of old baseball players, including Christy Mathewson. Take away a *y* from Christy and you have Christ, which is about the way baseball fans thought of Matty. "Matty was master of them all," the old line goes, and it's true. No other pitcher of the day dominated like Mathewson, or was more revered for it.

"Sometimes when you look at an old tobacco card of Christy Mathewson you'd swear you were looking down into the pure white soul, the yarn-wound core of baseball itself," Kit Kiefer wrote in *Baseball Cards* magazine not too long ago, and it's true of Mathewson's candy cards, too. Look at his E102 and you'll get the same feeling. You just have to pay less for the feeling, that's all.

The E102 set places before us a diamond little card, like the Mathewson, then dumps the leavings of a mystery. The cards lack identification; the backs carry the phrase, "This picture is one in a Set of Twenty-five BASE BALL PLAYERS, as follows,'' and a checklist, and nothing else. Whoever made the E102 set forgot to leave his name at the front desk.

There are indeed 25 players in the E102 set, but 28 different cards. There are extra poses of Larry Doyle, Dots Miller and Honus Wagner. The Dots Miller card was discovered only recently. These discoveries happen with candy cards at the rate of one about every two or three years. More discoveries probably will be made.

The E102 Mathewson, like a lot of semi-esoteric early issues of Hall of Famers, will go up in value right along without setting any world acceleration records. If you buy a properly graded example, you'll be able to sell it for more than you paid for it. And for the enjoyment you should derive from it, that's sufficient.

Paul's Score: 30

Kit's Score: 33

TOTAL SCORE: 63

1911 T201
Doublefolder
Cobb/Crawford

44

ow much more do you think a card ought to be worth because it's neat? Is neatness better than hipness? And what about coolness? Is 10 percent too low a coolness premium? If a baseball card could die and come back to life as a '57 Chevy, which card would it be? And which card would come back as the pair of Ray-bans?

Investors ought to ask themselves these questions. Collectors ought to know. Information is your greatest asset.

Okay, here are the answers. Take these down. Triplefolders get reincarnated as '57 Chevys. The '53 Bowmans get reincarnated as James Dean. And T201 Doublefolders come back as Ray-bans.

T201 Doublefolders rank exceptionally high on the neatness scale, which isn't one of our scales this time through but did figure prominently in this book's previous incarnation, *100 Bossest Baseball Cards Of All Time*. They're sort of Woody Guthrie Visits Spring Training, if that makes any sense. American originals. The little guy on the stick that dances the jig on top of a freshly cut tree stump. An Abe Lincoln mechanical bank. A leg-hold-trap wall clock. Jazz. Doublefolders are like that.

Doublefolders were a neat idea when they were first made. They were still a neat idea in 1955, when Topps stole the idea and made a Doublefolder set (Topps called them Doubleheaders) of its own. The idea in 1911 was to have two players share one pair of legs, legs being a precious commodity in turn-of-the-century baseball. When open, the card has a full-length picture of a ballplayer, all neatly proportioned and cut into frying-size pieces. When closed, the card shows a second ballplayer, bending over or crouching or doing whatever the other person's legs allow him to do. It's like one of those great old incredible-two-headed-monster movies, only from the shins up.

Another thing that makes the Doublefolders neat is that they were the first cards to include statistics on the card backs. Since the Doublefolders have considerably more back to play with than other tobacco cards, it made sense back then to burn up the space with some incidental hitting and fielding numbers. Nearly 80 years later we're still trying to figure out a better way to burn up space on the back of a baseball card. The T201 Doublefolders are responsible for taking innocent cigarette-smoking, tobacco-chewing, candy-scarfing baseball-card collectors and making numbers junkies out of them. The shame.

Doublefolders feature some great old ballplayers who don't make that many card appearances (Ed Walsh and Iron Man Joe McGinnity). You'll also find Frank Chance and Johnny Evers on one card (Joe Tinker couldn't—ouch—leg it out), Eddie Collins and Home Run Baker sharing one pair of legs, and Ty Cobb and Wahoo Sam Crawford, different as night and day, stuck on the same pair of pins like Chang and Eng, and joined at the tibia.

Doublefolders are reasonably priced and there's a good supply of them on the market, but it's an active market, so prices are going up. Two years ago a T201 Cobb-Crawford was $250. In the summer of '89, it was $400. Now it's $750 and accelerating.

People like Doublefolders. They want to buy Doublefolders. They'll want to buy the Cobb-Crawford Doublefolder first. You really ought to beat them to it.

Paul's Score: 31

Kit's Score: 32

TOTAL SCORE: 63

1955 Topps
Sandy Koufax

"SANDY" KOUFAX pitcher BROOKLYN DODGERS

45

Most of this book is full of unsung card heroes, cards that aren't worth what they should be worth for whatever reason. Here's a story of a card that is worth more than it should be worth but is worth it anyway. It's a changeup story of a fastball pitcher named Sandy Koufax.

We're not going to demean Koufax's performance by saying Bob Gibson was as fast, and was faster longer, or that Nolan Ryan was faster than either of them, or that Juan Marichal may have been better, or that even Jim Maloney was as dominant for about as long as Koufax. You can look up all that stuff, and debunk as many heroes as you want, on your own time. But gee whiz, Koufax had only four or five good years, and though they were great years, some of the greatest years ever by any pitcher, does his rookie card really deserve to be a $600 card solely on the strength of those years?

Look at the criteria. Koufax was in the right place at the right time. He pitched in New York and Los Angeles. With Don Drysdale he formed the most publicized one-two pitching punch in history. He was the ultimate strikeout pitcher, which is the pitching equivalent of being the ultimate home-run hitter. He was capable of reaching the headlines with a no-hitter or a perfect game in every start. And he quit when he was on the absolute top of his game. It doesn't matter that Koufax won only 165 games in his career because people don't remember that he won only 165 games in his career. All they remember is that amazing stretch of five years when Koufax was the dominant figure in baseball.

And there's the answer to your question. When someone buys a baseball card or puts a price on a baseball card, they're buying or pricing memories, not numbers. In many cases the memories and the numbers match up. In other cases—as in Koufax's case—the numbers and the memories don't quite match up. For his career, Koufax was not the greatest pitcher ever. But for a few years he was. And a few years are all that's necessary.

That's all that's been necessary to keep the Koufax card among the 1950s' top rookie cards, anyway. His '55 Topps card is the most valuable regular-run card of any pitcher in the 1950s (except for the 1951 Bowman Whitey Ford, which is a $1,000 card mainly because it's the first card in the set) and the second most valuable regular-run pitcher's card of the postwar era, trailing only the high-number '67 Topps Tom Seaver, which has a $750 catalog value but a corrected value of around $100. Its price has not backed off any, either; the '55 Koufax was a $125 card two years ago.

If the '55 Koufax hasn't weakened yet, it isn't going to weaken. His records will never be broken because to a large extent they're mental records. Compared to other cards in the set— with the exception of the Roberto Clemente rookie card, which reflects its share of mental records, too—the Koufax card is overvalued. But you can't convince anyone of that, and so it's not overvalued at all.

Paul's Score: 27

Kit's Score: 36

TOTAL SCORE: 63

T207 Buck Weaver

46

Buck Weaver was neither the luckiest man on the face of the earth nor the unluckiest cur ever to play the national game. He was probably at the wrong place at the wrong time, but hardly more than that. But that wrong place was in Chicago with the White Sox, and the wrong time was 1919, and because he was there then Weaver was banned from baseball for life.

What makes it so ironic is that Buck Weaver hit .324 in the 1919 World Series that he was accused of fixing, and he never received a cent for his alleged role in the fix. Buck Weaver went wrong, according to Commissioner Kenesaw Mountain Landis, when he sat in on a meeting regarding the fix and never reported that to authorities.

Weaver's luck had hardly been better early in his career, when as a shortstop he fielded poorly and hit medium-lousy. Five years of that sort of mediocrity were followed by four years of brilliance at the plate and at third base, his new position. So great were his skills that when Ty Cobb was asked who was the best third baseman of all time Cobb would vacillate. "Pie Traynor," he'd say sometimes. "Buck Weaver," the others.

But perhaps Weaver's luck is finally changing. With the movie *Eight Men Out* and the vigorous lobbying campaign for the restoration of Joe Jackson to a baseball throne, there has been solid demand for Buck Weaver's cards. The passage of time ought to intensify that. The only problem is finding a Weaver card.

With Joe Jackson the classic Cracker Jack card will do just fine. For Weaver the less classic T207 has to suffice.

The good news about the T207 set is that it's one of the big three tobacco sets. The bad news is that it's the least available, least understood, least appreciated and least collected of the three.

The problem with T207s used to be that they were so much more expensive than T206s and T205s (the other two of the big three), but recent big-gasp price gains for those sets have pretty much eliminated that distinction. Now the problem with T207s is that they look dull compared to the other two. They always did. The brown backgrounds placed behind players' heads make the players look like they're swimming in a sea of army drab. And once the brown backgrounds crease, they're done for. What looks like a light crease on other tobacco cards looks like a four-lane highway on a T207, and once that four-lane gets in there, McDonald's creases pop up and Motel 8 creases and K mart creases, and pretty soon your card doesn't look like a card any more but Des Moines just off the Interstate.

A real nice T207 Buck Weaver is a real challenge. It'll cost money and it'll be hard to find, but it'll reward you. And if the efforts to clear Jackson succeed and vindicate Weaver too, it might reward you greatly.

Paul's Score: 32

Kit's Score: 31

TOTAL SCORE: 63

1959 Topps
Stan Musial

47

I n the Milwaukee paper recently there was a piece on the time Red Sox pitcher Gene Conley and his roomie, the definitely immortal Pumpsie Green, went AWOL from the Bosox, ditched a cab in a traffic jam, greatly aided the gross profits of a nearby liquor store, tried to check into the Shoreham Hotel without luggage, and were finally tracked down trying to catch a plane to Israel. The reason the two decided on Israel supposedly had something to do with Pumpsie's given first name (Elijah) and the name of Israel's national airline (El Al), but Conley says he's still not sure why they did it. It was just one of those things that happens when a pitcher and infielder wind up in a cab together.

Like what happened to Stan Musial in baseball-card land. Musial appeared in the 1953 Bowman color set and then went AWOL and didn't appear again until the 1959 Topps set. Contracts were the reason why, but we don't know whether there was a contract with Bowman and Musial that didn't revert to Topps with the change in ownership, or whether Musial chose not to re-up with Bowman or sign with Topps. Musial was certainly not averse to appearing on cards. He appeared on Red Man chewing-tobacco and Hunter hot-dog cards while he was out of the big sets, though he appeared on no cards whatsoever from 1956–57. Maybe he just felt about bubble gum the way Honus Wagner felt about tobacco.

Whatever the contractual hangups that kept Musial out of sets, he made a surprise appearance in the 1958 Topps all-star subset, then made his triumphant return in the 1959 set. The card is the perfect Stan Musial card: a cheery Polish face, with pierogi dimples and a Little Wally polka smile set in a circle on a sky-blue background, with tight lower-case letters skittering up to one corner. It's not cheap at $100, but considering how long he had been away and how few nice Stan Musial cards are out there, it's a good card to have.

It's a good card to hold, too. Three years ago it was a $24 card; in early 1988 it was a $35 card. And since it's not very difficult to locate in well-centered, high-grade condition, it's the sort of card everyone can buy and everyone wants.

Musial's missing-person status through the middle of the 1950s is even more frustrating than Ted Williams' on-again, off-again appearances. Even when Williams wasn't in a Topps or Bow-man he could be found in a Red Man set or on a Wilson franks card. But Musial totally vanished for two years. Those years can't be made up, and this card can't help bring them back. But it's not supposed to.

Paul's Score: 28

Kit's Score: 34

TOTAL SCORE: 62

1955 Topps
Harmon Killebrew

48

You want to talk about one-dimensional players? They really don't come with less dimension than Harmon Killebrew.

Killebrew couldn't hit for average, but he hit 573 home runs, playing in parks that weren't exactly hitters' paradises. Only Babe Ruth hit more among American League ballplayers. Killebrew was slow as a school bus, but he hit 573 home runs. He played three positions (first base, third base and the outfield) and couldn't really field well at any of them, but he hit 573 home runs. He led his teams—usually mediocre teams—to only one World Series in 22 seasons, but he hit 573 home runs. Harmon Killebrew was elected to the Hall of Fame because he hit 573 home runs.

That's all right; plenty of one-dimensional ballplayers are in the Hall of Fame, and there'll be a few more when the likes of Nolan Ryan and Reggie Jackson are elected. The problem with Killebrew is there's nothing to remember. Reggie left us with a score of Mr. October blasts, moon shots he just stood and watched, loud strikeouts to remember him by; Ryan left us with strikeout after strikeout and memories of a scatterarmed kid turned into a fireballing surgeon. Killebrew left us with nothing.

But some people remember lying on the floor with a bottle of cream soda watching Killebrew in between Hamm's beer commercials, and listening to Merle Harmon and Halsey Hall, and watching Killebrew send another of those 573 home runs screaming and spinning into a Minnesota mosquito night. And some people can't understand why Killebrew's card isn't worth more.

Some people could be right. Next to the Koufax rookie at $600 and the Clemente rookie at $900 the Killebrew looks cheap at $250. In constant dollars it's worth less than the 1954 Topps Kaline and Banks rookies. But the Killebrew card carries a higher corrected value than the 1948 Bowman Yogi Berra, and when Clemente's rookie card is corrected for high-number inflation, it's only slightly more valuable than the Killebrew. In all fairness to Killer fans everywhere, the card's fully valued, not underpriced, and only as good a buy as any card in the 1955 Topps set.

Of course, the 1955 Topps set is a good set. It's gone up about two and a half times in the last 14 months. And the Killebrew card is a cute thing. The Killer looks about as young as one of

145

Jerry Lee Lewis' brides, and sleepy as a newborn calf. This is not the face of someone who would slug 573 home runs, and that makes the card all the more desirable because of it.

Killebrew was a one-dimensional player, but a big one dimension, no question about it. And he looks pretty good when you subject his card to some one-dimensional analysis. But as soon as you add the other dimensions you get a better insight into the real Killebrew. And you know what? He still looks pretty good.

Paul's Score: 27

Kit's Score: 35

TOTAL SCORE: 62

Old Judge
Old Hoss Radbourn

49

L augh all you want. A pitcher named after a piece of decrepit livestock, a candidate for the glue factory, a cowboy's worn-out friend. Go ahead and laugh, but remember that pitcher Charles "Old Hoss" Radbourn did some things that are hard to imagine under any rules, including Little League.

Consider his 1884 season. Actually, you might call it his 1884 career. Old Hoss started 73 games and finished each and every one of them. Pitching for Providence of the National League, Radbourn won 60 games and lost 12. History has lost the 73rd game for us. He had an earned-run average of 1.38, and even recorded a relief win and a save. Say what you will, but that's the definitive career year.

Certainly the rules were different in those days. The distance from home plate to the pitcher's mound was 50 feet. Batters could ask for high strikes or low strikes. But the numbers neither helped nor hindered Radbourn. He simply pitched virtually every game his team played—30 of 32—until Providence clinched the pennant.

Radbourn won 302 games in his career, and was one of the first players elected to the Hall of Fame. His cards, what cards there are, are reasonably affordable, though they are worth about as much as what Radbourn was paid for his 60-game season.

That's not that much, surprisingly. Just about any collector can afford a Radbourn card, given sort of a head shot at it. The problem is finding a card to buy.

One place to look is the Old Judge set. It's sort of a misnomer, calling the Old Judge set a set. It's more a sprawling mess of subsets and variations. There are only 117 different players in the set, but the number of varieties and variations stretch into the thousands. The set takes up 13 pages in the *Standard Catalog Of Baseball Cards*.

Old Judges are photographs glued to blank-backed pieces of cardboard. The pictures, taken in the studio of Brooklyn photographer Joseph Hall, were rarely reproduced in great numbers and were of marginal quality at best. The poses took liberties with reality, too; on the cards, balls hang from ceilings, runners avoid tags while both players face the camera, and batters swing with the ferocity of ladybugs.

To anyone who collects Hall of Famers, Old Judges are vital. If you need a card of King Kelly, Old Hoss or most any other Hall of Famer of the 1880s, the Old Judge set is the best place to go looking for them.

Old Judges are too scarce to streak upward in value, but their scarcity ensures they'll never fall. That's reassuring, and the cards themselves are fascinating. Old Hoss is no laugher, that's for sure.

Paul's Score: 28

Kit's Score: 34

TOTAL SCORE: 62

1969 Topps
Reggie Jackson

50

Sometimes it's hard to grasp that there was a time, not so very long ago, when the baseball-card business was nothing like it is today.

That time is actually anytime before 1981, when real competition changed the business forever. Before 1981 there was no premium for rookie cards, and no real need to cram as many rookies as possible into a set. In 1990 the entire starting lineup of the Columbus Mudcats is on a major-league baseball card somewhere, either as a Major League Prospect or Rated Rookie or Rookie Prospect or Star Rookie or Future Star.

(Did you know you can create your own rookie subset at home? It's fun and easy, and so educational. Just take the words and phrases "Hot," "Major League," "Rookie," "Star," "Future," "Tomorrow's," and "1989," and put them in one column, and take the words and phrases "Prospect," "Rookie," "Star," and "Career Minor Leaguer," and put them in a second column. Then just match one phrase from the first column with a phrase from the second. Paste them to a card of any A-ball minor leaguer, and there you have it.)

That's why it's hard for us to sit in 1990 and look back at the Topps 1969 Reggie Jackson card. Jackson had taken Topps completely by surprise in 1968, which is a surprise for us and our hot-rookie mentalities. Reggie had appeared in 35 games with the Kansas City A's in 1967, and while he didn't set any land-speed records with his hitting (.178, one home run), he was a former high first-round draft pick, and at least he was up with the big club. Even back then, Topps put all sorts of players on rookie cards whose entire major-league career consisted of one inning or one at-bat, and put Marv Staehle alone on at least 10 or 12 rookie cards, but it couldn't figure out that Reggie Jackson might make the majors someday.

Of course, there was no pressure on it to do so. If Topps missed Reggie Jackson in 1968 it could go back and pick him up in 1969, which it did. Collectors wouldn't abandon Topps for another card company because it didn't have a Reggie Jackson card, because there was no other company to abandon Topps for. Funny how monopolies work that way.

Right on schedule, Topps came out with a Reggie Jackson card in its 1969 set. It's a good card of a great ballplayer, and about your only chance to see Reggie stripped of his trademark brashness (except for the 1973 Topps Reggie, which shows Jackson in the outfield about to throw up). It's a $300 card, and not a bad buy at that price. You can count on that price to go up as induction day nears for Jackson.

Maybe it would be interesting to be collecting in 1990 and have seven different Reggie Jackson rookie cards to choose from. But maybe it's better—and more lucrative—this way.

Paul's Score: 25

Kit's Score: 36

TOTAL SCORE: 61

1972 Topps
Carlton Fisk/
Cecil Cooper

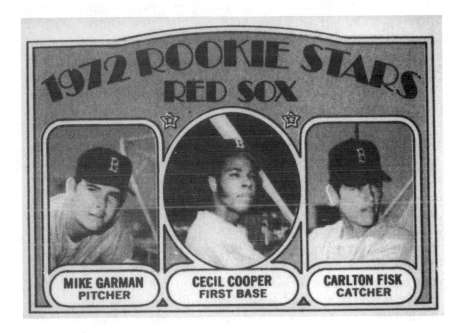

51

Weren't we just talking about ballplayers who are destined for Cooperstown, whether we think about them getting there or not? Sure we were. We always are. The next name we'd like to throw out for your consideration is Carlton Fisk.

There's probably more agreement on the Hall of Fame potential of Carlton Fisk than there was on Bert Blyleven or some other names we'll throw out later. Fisk has turned out to be the dominant catcher of the 1980s. He's caught more games than Johnny Bench, has a higher lifetime batting average and will have more hits, and is closing in on some of the batting records that sped Bench into the Hall on the first ballot. Fisk is responsible for one of the game's most dramatic moments, his 12th-inning homer in the sixth game of the 1975 World Series that Fisk kept fair through force of will. He's played 19 years and hit 20 or more home runs nine times. His career .270 batting average is not the highest in creation, but it's 20 points more than respectable for a catcher, and three points higher than Bench's career average. Fisk, when and if he ever retires, will leave the game as one of its all-time great catchers, an equal of Cochrane, Dickey, Campanella and Bench.

So if that's the case—and it is—why is his rookie card only $50? Granted, it's an ugly card from a buck-toothed set, but that's *de rigeur* for rookie cards. My gosh, if you can't have an ugly rookie card what's the sense of having a rookie card at all? It's not like he shares the card with Adolf Hitler and Idi Amin, either. Mike Garman, a halfway fair pitcher, is on the card along with Fisk and Cecil Cooper. And Cooper was an excellent major-league ballplayer on his way to Cooperstown right with Fisk until he lost track of his batting stroke 15 years into his career. Still, Cooper finished with 2,192 hits and a .298 career average. That should be enough to give Cooper a $12, 17-year-old rookie card by himself. But you throw in Fisk and total it up and it only comes to $50. It just doesn't make sense.

Does that mean you should buy this card? Yes. Immediately. Sell all your children, call up the place that buys dead-and-down livestock and have them come take away your wife or husband for cash, take your '89 T-Bird to the auto-parts salvage yard and take whatever they'll give you for it, stock up on macaroni and cheese, and use whatever money you can scrape together from all that to buy Fisk rookie cards. Is that strong enough for you? This is a good card, a nice card, a wonderful card, an ugly card, but a card you should have. And if you don't get it now and decide you want it later on when it's $100, that's your own darn fault.

Paul's Score: 24

Kit's Score: 36

TOTAL SCORE: 60

R-312
Joe DiMaggio

52

The Joe DiMaggio rookie card. Everyone knows which card's the Joe DiMaggio rookie card. It's the '38 Goudey, right? Nope. '41 Play Ball? Nope. Not the Zeenut PCL card? Nope. Not the Zeenut PCL card. If we tell you you're not going to believe us, so we won't tell you right away.

How about that Joe DiMaggio, huh? To a generation he was the epitome of style. He did the little things so well. He cut the second-base bag like a diamond cutter slicing up the Hope crystal. Legend has it that he never missed a cutoff man. He glided in the outfield. He played his last days in the same high style despite tremendous pain because, as he told a teammate, "There might be someone in the stands out there who's never seen me play." He married Marilyn Monroe and loved her to the end. They called him "The Yankee Clipper," after the sleek, elegant, faster-than-fast sailing ship, and DiMaggio was every bit of that.

The DiMaggio mystique remains intact. If anything, the years have made him even larger than life. His reputation rubbed off on the savings and loans and coffeemakers he pitched. Like a wonderful seasoning, DiMaggio seems to improve everything he touches, and the autograph of an aging DiMaggio has become the hobby's toughest ticket.

Rookie cards were a foreign concept in the 1930s, but the acknowledged first DiMaggio card is in the '38 Goudey Heads-Up set. It's an interesting and desirable card, and it probably deserves its rather lofty price tag.

But the '38 Goudey is not the first DiMaggio card. In fact, DiMaggio had appeared on several cards before 1938. One of the cards he graced—and DiMaggio did everything with grace—was a 1936 R-312.

You can question whether it's proper to call the R-312 the DiMaggio rookie, but it comes as close as any. Its competition consists of either multiple-player cards or Canadian issues, and few are widely available.

The R-312 DiMaggio is one of the better cards in this rather mixed lot. It incorrectly spells DiMaggio "DiMagio," and like all R-312s it's just a tinted, blank-backed black-and-white photograph, but it's attractive and large, a real showpiece.

Perhaps this card's best trait is that it's the classic DiMaggio picture, showing Joe at the end of his long, fluid swing. This photograph was the basis for the ultimate DiMaggio card, the 1941 Play Ball, and it's the image of greatness we all want to preserve.

It's hard to imagine anything diminishing DiMaggio's legend. Death won't. DiMaggio's death should only improve the market for his cards. High prices for his cards are the inevitable result, but for the time being the R-312 is an unknown classic, relatively cheap by DiMaggio standards. If it remains that way, it'll be a wonderful opportunity to have and hold an impressive card of the ever-impressive—and ever-graceful—DiMaggio.

Paul's Score: 28

Kit's Score: 32

TOTAL SCORE: 60

1932 U.S. Caramel
Fred Lindstrom

CHARLES (LINDY) LINDSTROM

53

Let's be blunt: the 1932 U.S. Caramel Lindstrom is a historically important and valuable card. But it is not a million-dollar card, or even a hundred-thousand-dollar card, or whatever figure its owner might care to come up with.

At the moment, the 1932 Fred "Lindy" Lindstrom card is a fairly recent discovery. A novelty. It fills a niche in hobby lore. It gives collectors something to talk about. Only one has ever been found, and a great deal of hoopla surrounded its discovery. The card is unique, so a little bit of hoopla would be appropriate. But the hype has overshadowed the card. The Lindstrom card needs to be considered on its own merits.

The 1932 U.S. Caramel set is a difficult set, and a historic one. As one of the last of the caramel-card sets, it's a key set in the shift from candy cards to gum cards. The cards are scarce, but they're hardly stunners. The limited supply has only a limited demand, though prices remain high.

The set is made up of "famous athletes," but 27 of the 32 cards in the set are baseball players, so essentially it's a baseball set. True to its name, the athletes are famous, even today: Cobb, Ruth, Gehrig, Hornsby, Dickey, 22 Hall of Famers in all.

But for a long time, the U.S. Carmel set was thought to contain cards of only 21 Hall of Famers, and was thought to be missing card #16. It wasn't unusual for sets to be missing numbers right in the middle of the set. Topps did it with its sets; so did Goudey. And any set where there was a premium offered for a complete set—like the U.S. Caramel set—was bound to have one or two cards scarce or nonexistent. It does save on the premiums. Though there were scattered rumors that card #16 was Fred Lindstrom, as is so often the case with early tobacco and gum cards, it was supposition.

The supposition ended in 1988 when a cancelled and voided Lindstrom card was found. It had been in a file at the U.S. Caramel company. Immediately it was dubbed "the million-dollar card," by its new owner, Joshua Evans. Other dealers pooh-poohed that claim: "It's not worth $25,000," one said, and others nodded their heads in agreement.

But is a card a million-dollar card simply because its owner says it's a million-dollar card, because it's unique at the moment? No, of course not. Supply and demand, market forces, create a million-dollar card, and if a card is unique there are no market forces because there can be no market. If no one besides the owner wants a unique item it has no special value. If five people want the item but none is willing to pay more than $100 for it, the item's real value is $100. The owner can ask a million dollars for it, but that fact alone does not make it a million-dollar item. Until someone pays $1 million for a Lindstrom card it has no market value, just a claimed market value. And there is serious doubt that the card would bring more than a top-grade T-206 Wagner if it were put on the market—sold at auction, perhaps.

The Lindstrom card is fascinating. It helped attract attention back to older cards at a time when the market was new-card crazy. But a million-dollar card? Only in advertising copy.

Paul's Score: 30

Kit's Score: 30

TOTAL SCORE: 60

1986 Donruss Rookies Bo Jackson

54

Speaking of faith in the unknown, here's some ideas of what to do with Bo Jackson, Mr. Unknown Quantity himself.

Scenario For A Nike Commercial #1: Bo Jackson steps to the plate like a lion getting ready for a blood meal. A quick cut to the scoreboard shows the score's tied, two out, 24th inning. Another quick cut shows two runners aboard, both bleary-eyed and heavy-legged and barely able to take another step. A third quick cut shows the pitcher, sweating heavily, chewing tobacco and spitting, swearing under his breath. Cut to the fog rolling in. Cut to large carrion-eating birds perching on the light standards. Cut to the pitcher's delivery. Cut to Jackson's swing. Cut to footage of nuclear explosion. Cut to Jackson trotting around bases. Cut to closeup of Jackson. Jackson says, "Just do it, baby." Show logo.

Scenario For A Nike Commercial #2: Open with Bo Jackson playing his normal left field. The park is Yellowstone. Cut to runner on third. Cut to hitter. Hitter drives one over Jackson's head, over Wyoming border, past Old Faithful and into Montana. Cut to Jackson running down ball. Show Jackson making the catch, wheeling and throwing ball. Show ball traveling 21.3 miles and arriving at home plate in time to nip the runner. Cut to closeup of Jackson. Close same as before.

Scenario For A Nike Commercial #3: Show Bo Jackson coming to plate like young lion approaching blood meal. Cut to pitcher, sweating, spitting, swearing, all profusely. Cut back to Bo whiffing on an 0–2 curveball in the dirt. Cut again to Bo swinging over a two-strike low breaking pitch. Cut once more to Bo, swinging behind in the count, on a bender. Cut finally to Bo cutting and missing on a big breaker after fouling off the pitcher's first two offerings. Close same as before.

Most people who buy Bo Jackson cards go for the first two scenarios and make believe that the third doesn't exist. But all three are Bo Jackson, and when you buy his card you get them all: the awesome hitter, the breathtaking fielder (the tremendous baserunner, we might add), and the strikeout king of the civilized world.

The funny thing is, when you put them all together you get Jose Canseco. For all the tall tales, true or partially true or not, that get told about Jose Canseco, the tales are even taller about Bo Jackson. Bo Jackson hitting the longest home run ever hit in

Kansas City. Bo Jackson hitting the longest home run ever hit in Seattle. Bo Jackson throwing a 300-foot BB to home plate to nail a baserunner tagging up from third. If Jose Canseco has the potential to be a 40–40 man year in and year out, Bo Jackson has the potential to be a 50–50 man.

So where are his cards? Why isn't Bo Jackson's card $55?

Bo Jackson doesn't have a card that could be $55, for one thing. It was a stroke of good fortune for Donruss that it picked Jose Canseco for its 1986 set. But when Heisman Trophy winner Bo Jackson shocked the football and baseball worlds by signing with the Royals, and when the Royals rushed him into Double-A, and then when the Royals rushed him to the majors, Donruss was caught a little off-guard. So Donruss did what any good American money-grubbing card company would: It put out a set whose sole purpose for being—almost—was Bo Jackson.

Donruss hadn't done an end-of-year set before 1986, and it's hard to say whether they ever would have done one if 1986 hadn't been such a remarkable year for rookies. In addition to Mr. Unknown Quantity Jackson, Wally Joyner, Ruben Sierra, Kevin Mitchell, Will Clark and Barry Bonds had come up and starred for their respective teams with no advance warning. Jose Canseco, even though he appeared on a regular Donruss card, had had a marvelous rookie season, and could always stand to be on another card. The demand for cards of rookies existed like it had never existed before, and who was Donruss to spit in the face of demand? So the hobby got its Donruss Rookies set, replete with cards of the year's big rookies, another card of Jose Canseco, and a hastily constructed card of Bo Jackson.

The card doesn't have much to say about Mr. Jackson's baseball career, and nothing at all to say about his pro career. It's the card of a football player in a baseball uniform, that's all it is. But it's one of Bo Jackson's two first cards (the other is in the '86 Topps Update set), and so it's significant.

It's also only $11, so if you believe Jackson will not give up baseball for football—and he'd be a fool to do it—or even if you don't, this is a card to have solely for the sheer potential of the player pictured. You don't want to be spending all your time chasing after cards with potential. This one you do.

• 1986 Donruss Rookies Bo Jackson •

Paul's Score: 24

Kit's Score: 36

TOTAL SCORE: 60

1989 Star Co.
Bob Hamelin

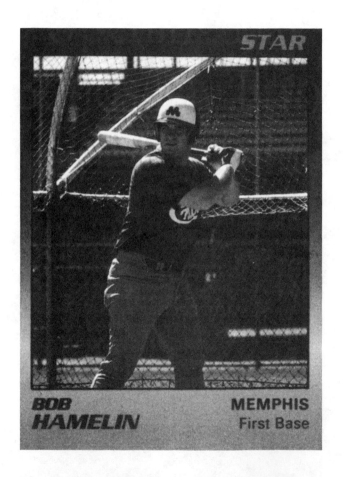

I t would be nice if all the great marketing ideas that ought to succeed really would succeed. Can you imagine a baseball-card world filled with plaks and doubleheaders and dice games and mini sets and team stickers? Yes. We live in one now.

Oh. Sorry.

One of the best kooky ideas of the last five years didn't come from Topps but from an outfit called Star International. Star got into the baseball-card business by making basketball cards, and then by making single-star sets. It'll make a Mike Schmidt set that consists of 12 or 14 cards or stickers with pictures of Mike on the fronts and a career synopsis on the backs. They're tolerable sets, except when the player is just starting out and there's no career to synopsize. They have a little value and generate a little collector interest, but nothing that would yank your head around.

In 1988 Star took its major-league licenses and entered the minor-league card market. Since it was the only minor-league cardmaker with major-league licenses, it could show team logos without having to worry about Major League Baseball jumping down its throat. Since it was already making cards with major-league printing quality, it was no sweat to make major-league-quality minor-league cards (an innovation in the minor-league-card market, where notebook filler paper was considered high-quality stock). And since it was already spending lots of money getting its licenses and dealing with players, it was no sweat to throw some money around and line up minor-league teams that wanted Star International sets.

Its first sets were well-received. They were the best-looking minor-league cards ever. So in 1989 it upped the ante a little more. It came out with minor-league cards in wax packs.

It's a devilishly brilliant idea, when you think about it. A set of 100 top minor-league prospects in wax packs. The ultimate wax-pack gamble. Not only are you gambling that you'll get a certain ballplayer, but you're also gambling that that certain minor-league ballplayer will turn out to be a great major-league ballplayer. People who think they know something about baseball ought to be in these cards up to their eyeballs.

One of the best gambles is a fellow named Bob "The Hammer" Hamelin. Hamelin was one of the last cuts off the 1988 U.S.

Olympic Baseball Team, and a second-round draft pick of the Kansas City Royals. He tore up the short-season Northwest League in a few months there, and made the big jump to Double-A Memphis in 1989. He has tremendous power, but he also hits for average and doesn't strike out much. He could be the power-hitting first baseman the Royals haven't had since John Mayberry.

But it's a gamble. Hamelin hasn't played a game above Triple-A as this is being written, and he may never. Any price that might be placed on his cards is purely arbitrary. But if you're willing to gamble, buy the Star Memphis set and the Pro Cards Memphis set, and then buy all the first-series minor-league wax packs you can, looking for Bob Hamelin cards. The poses in Star's sets are different from the poses on Star's wax-pack cards, so you do need some of both. Don't spend too much money, have fun, and do tip your hat to Star International for devising a neat idea at a time when neat ideas have been sort of baked out of the hobby.

Paul's Score: 30

Kit's Score: 30

TOTAL SCORE: 60

1953 Bowman
Pee Wee Reese

56

A fellow, a good writer, a writer for a major metropolitan magazine, submitted a manuscript recently to *Baseball Cards* magazine. All he could do for the first three or four paragraphs—long paragraphs—was marvel at the beauty of the 1953 Bowman Pee Wee Reese card. He didn't resort to any comparisons between this card and the *Mona Lisa* or a Van Gogh sunflower or *Guernica*, thank goodness, but he did use the term "pure art" at least twice.

It's bunk in a sense, total and utter bunk, but in another sense it's something quite wonderful. A baseball card must be awfully good for a thoughtful, composed fellow to start gushing over it as if it were the Sistine ceiling. But '53 Bowmans can do that.

There's never been a more beautiful baseball-card set than the 1953 Bowman set. While the cards are hardly high art or pure art or folk art or even bubble-gum art, they are quite a sight to see. And the Pee Wee Reese card, which freezes the Dodger shortstop four feet above the second-base bag, head turned towards first and arm sure to follow, is undoubtedly one of the most beautiful of the beautiful.

There is something to be said for beauty in this hobby, you know. It isn't all just dollars and cents. That's why collectors are such avid buyers of '53 Bowmans. They call them "pure cards," not because every other card is impure, but because collectors love the *look*, the uncluttered fronts, the deep photographs and the vibrant colors, the unmatched evocation of a mood. Baseball is one of the few sports that lends itself as well to portrait photography as action photography, and the photos on the '53 Bowmans are simply the best examples of portrait photography of 1950s ballplayers you can find. They rival the baseball portraits of the great 1920s and 1930s baseball photographer Charles Martin Conlan. Nostalgia doesn't get any prettier than this.

And maybe it's no coincidence, but '53 Bowmans have been a great buy over the last several years. The Reese card more than tripled in value in a year and a half. Other '53 Bowmans have posted similar gains. The set is up about 220 percent in the last two years. It's the old unholy triangle of supply, beauty and demand. If the cards are out there, and they're beautiful, and people want them, their values will increase right along. It's always a pleasure to know that you can make money by collecting what you love. The '53 Bowman Pee Wee Reese is proof of that pleasure.

• 1953 Bowman Pee Wee Reese •

Paul's Score: 29

Kit's Score: 31

TOTAL SCORE: 60

1987 Donruss Opening Day Bonds/Ray Error

57

To the people who believe that valuable cards aren't made anymore, the authors wish to respectfully offer a reply: phpff-pffphphft.

Valuable cards are being made every day, and all it takes is a little intelligence to track them down.

For instance, smart people know that in 1987 Donruss issued its one and only Opening Day set. The set contained one card for each member of each team's Opening Day starting lineup, and was sold as a complete set in a fruitcake-style, plastic covered box. The set followed strict Donruss guidelines: Don't make any of your sets look any different from any of your other sets, except for the color of the borders. Save wear and tear on the design staff, create impressions of continuity, enhance recognizability, and induce deep sleep. Wring out and use over and over again, like a Handi-Wipe with statistics.

Early on in the life cycle of the Donruss Opening Day set a collector (and it's always a collector who notices these things) noticed that the card of Barry Bonds in his set didn't show Barry Bonds at all but Johnny Ray. Well, he told the company, and the company, as it should, immediately stopped production, corrected the error, and didn't tell anyone about what they'd done. When the hobby press stopped to inquire, Donruss was very up-front about it. Yes, they said, they had corrected the Bonds card, and corrected it early. Fewer than one-tenth of 1 percent of the press run was wrong, and they were happy the number was that low.

For a matter of fact, so were collectors. You might have thought that the announcement that such a small number of sets were wrong might have started a run on the sets, but it didn't happen. People just didn't buy the sets. The concept was all right, but the timing was wrong. Collectors were too caught up in buying regular wax packs and completing sets to care much about buying a 264-card set in addition to that. The set's been a drag on the market ever since. Today you can still buy a complete, sealed Donruss Opening Day set for about $10–$12, and it might have the Bonds-Ray error in it, too.

The Bonds-Ray error is the rarest card made by a major manufacturer in the 1980s, and one of the rarest of all time. A dealer in Iowa advertised he was buying the cards for months, and only came up with a handful. Krause Publications' chief

cataloger and price-guide coordinator did the same thing, and
came up with four or five. He auctioned off a couple, and got
around $200 each for them. The catalog value on the card is
$125, but if you were ever able to find one chances are you'd
have to pay twice or three times that.

You can tell the Barry Bonds error card from the correct card by
the color of Bonds' jersey. If the player is wearing a white jersey
it's Bonds; if he's wearing a dark jersey it's Ray.

Since unopened sets are still around everywhere, it's a mystery
to us why more people don't just buy the sets on the chance
they might have the error card inside. But it doesn't happen,
and so the rarest card of the '80s just keeps getting rarer.

There aren't many error cards you could really call significant,
even if you were to go back to the turn of the century looking
for them. This card is significant. It's about as good a buy as you
can find, even if it costs you a couple hundred dollars. At least
we think so.

Paul's Score: 25

Kit's Score: 35

TOTAL SCORE: 60

1969 Topps
White-Letter
Mickey Mantle

58

The reason collectors like errors on baseball cards so much is because errors prove to collectors that the card companies are as dumb as the collectors always thought they were. Would a smart company let a photo of Bob Uecker batting left-handed— or better yet, Hank Aaron batting left-handed—go through? Would a smart company trade Bump Wills to the Blue Jays without telling him? Would a smart company paint a uniform on Mike Laga that makes him look like the definitive mound of strawberry-marshmallow seafoam salad with a Mike Laga head on top? And would a smart company make a little mistake, like putting the names on a card in white letters instead of yellow, and then go to great lengths to correct it, so everyone will know what a big mistake they made?

Topps is a smart company. They have made millions and millions of dollars selling baseball cards. But . . .

No.

In 1969 Topps made quite a few more errors and created more variations than it had in any other set that decade. It airbrushed out logos halfway, then went back and airbrushed them out completely. It left little loops of type on some cards, then went back and removed the loops. It issued cards of Donn Clendenon with the Expos and the Astros, and cards of Clay Dalrymple with the Phillies and Orioles. It issued a card of Aurelio Rodriguez that actually showed a 12-year-old batboy (this from a smart company?). And in its biggest series of little errors, it issued 26 cards where the players' names can be found in either yellow or white. It's the least-known run of errors in contemporary major card sets, and one of the most valuable.

Some of the white-letter variations are harder to find than others, and some are much more valuable, depending on the player being white-lettered. Willie McCovey's white-letter card, for instance, is $90. Bobby Bolin's card is $10, same as the other white-letter commons, but his card is much harder to find with white letters than the card of, say, Paul Casanova.

It just so happened that the card of Mickey Mantle fell in the 426–512 white-letter/yellow-letter number series. It just so happened that the card is Mantle's last regular card. And it furthermore just so happened that Mickey Mantle's card is one of those that came with either white letters or yellow letters. The result is the most expensive regular-set Mantle card of the decade, the most expensive non-rookie card of the decade, and one of the most desirable cards of the decade.

Most error cards have a market limited to the people who understand what the error is, why it's important, and why you just can't have one of these correct ones over here. And, granted, a lot of casual collectors are going to have some trouble understanding why they have to spend $475 for a card that has Mantle's name in white letters when there's a perfectly good yellow-letter Mantle over there for $175. But Mantle transcends the usual rules. People will spend $475 for a white-letter Mantle because it's Mantle, not necessarily because they understand that white-letter variations are 15 to 20 times scarcer than the correct yellow-letter varieties.

People will also spend $475 for a white-letter Mantle because they realize the card has tripled in value in the last two-plus years. The combination of marquee value and scarcity is just a little too good to pass up.

Mantle is always a sure buy. Error cards, once the scarcity of the error is known, are always a good buy. The combination of the two is incendiary.

Paul's Score: 22

Kit's Score: 37

TOTAL SCORE: 59

1986 Donruss
Jose Canseco

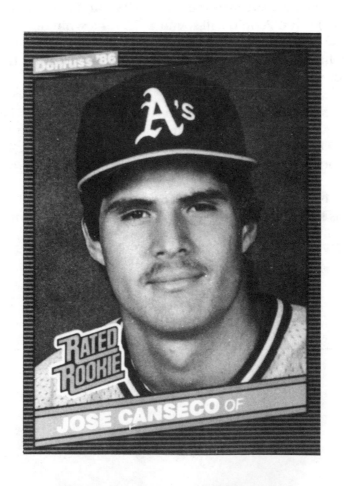

59

I n late 1988, just before Jose Canseco didn't lead the Oakland Athletics to the World Championship, 1986 Jose Canseco cards were trading for $75 and up. Each.

Was there any reason for it? Was there any earthly, logical reason why the two-year-old, not-scarce cards of an unproven hitter should have been selling for more than the first cards of some Hall of Famers?

No. None whatsoever.

Let's rephrase that. Yes. Plenty of reasons.

Jose Canseco represents the absurd high end of the baseball-card market. There's no reason that a three-year-old, not-scarce Jose Canseco card should trade for $75 or even $55 (its current value), when you judge it by the standards by which you judge other baseball cards. Jose Canseco had one good year (1986), one off year (1987), one very good year (1988), and one pretty good year (1989), and it adds up to $55. The old Ted Williams standard—if a guy's really good, let him do it five years in a row—is nowhere to be found, the Dwight Gooden rule that personal problems can have an impact on anyone's cards is right out the window, the better-than-the-stock-market philosophy of linearity—what you see on the field today is what you will see in the baseball-card market tomorrow—is way gone. This card is breaking all the conventions, and doing it on the high side, where conventions traditionally aren't broken in the baseball-card biz.

There's a reason why the Jose Canseco card rose beyond all reasonable limits, and continues to hold its value when it really shouldn't anymore. The reason is faith.

Faith is the wrong commodity to try and measure in an investment situation, because usually in investment situations faith doesn't do any good. Investors buy a stock and hope it will go up in value. They have faith it will go up in value. They tell their spouse over toast and coffee it will go up in value. It doesn't, and all the hoping in the neighborhood and all the faith in the world that that stock is going to go up isn't going to make it go up.

But when someone buys an '86 Donruss Canseco card (it doesn't matter when) and has faith it will go up in value, it's a different kind of faith. She bought that card because she believes Jose Canseco will be one of the most awesome players the game has ever known. She believes Canseco will shatter batting records that were previously thought shatterproof, that Canseco will hit home runs in bunches and steal bases in clusters and drive in runs the way Gehrig used to. She believes Canseco will be the key player in a new Oakland dynasty, and lead his team to even more divisional titles and loop flags and World Series victories. *And she's not alone.* Millions of people around the country, little kids on street corners who saved some favorite cards out of a few wax packs and high schoolers at card shows and suit-and-tie types who call what they do with baseball cards ''assembling a portfolio'' believe the very same thing: Jose Canseco will be great. No matter how much his card costs now, it will cost more later. There are other players who are capable of generating faith like that—Gregg Jefferies comes to mind first—but no one is capable of making people believe quite like Jose Canseco.

Canseco doesn't deserve it. Despite a great 1988 he's still largely an unproven talent, Bo Jackson writ large. His card doesn't deserve it, either. According to the rules of the market, all faith aside, his '86 Donruss card ought to be tanking it right now. Ask yourself if Canseco's rookie card ought to be $55, and see what you come up with.

If you don't like faith, don't buy this card. But if you believe, this one's all yours.

Paul's Score: 22

Kit's Score: 37

TOTAL SCORE: 59

1973 Topps
Dwight Evans

wight Evans is one of those ballplayers who seems to get much better with age. He has always been able to field his position better than anyone in baseball; one of the sure things at Fenway Park, besides the Red Sox finding *some* way to screw things up in the end, is that baserunners don't take liberties with Dwight Evans' arm in right field. They don't underestimate his glove or his range, either. And after 17 years Evans is just assumed to be great out there. And for the most part he is.

Evans ended the 1989 season with around 2,300 hits and 375 home runs, and a .274 batting average. Match that up with a .373 on-base percentage and his definitive defensive abilities and all of a sudden Evans looks like a true Hall of Famer—a real sure thing.

You might say that. You might also say Evans will have to hit .300 two or three times more, and hit 70 more home runs, before Cooperstown will take him absolutely seriously. But if you think that will happen—and it's certainly possible—then Evans' rookie card bears a little checking into.

When you check into it, you'll find Evans appears on a 1973 Rookie Outfielders card with not-bad outfielders Al Bumbry and Charlie Spikes. It catalogs at $40 now. Two years ago it cataloged at between $7 and $10.50. This card isn't fooling anyone. If it were a pitcher it would have been yanked two innings ago.

But that's good. Price movement at modest price levels like these is good. It shows that the card will move up, and because there's a Mike Schmidt rookie one card away sitting at $300, it shows that there's still quite a ways yet for the card to move.

And it will probably move more, and take out a chunk of that $300, before it's finished. Evans in '89 showed no signs of backing off from his Cooperstown pace, and as long as he keeps doing that—and with the way Evans' performances have improved with age, that could be forever—his card will not weaken, and will continue to outperform the set as a whole by at least 100 percent.

It's true, but it's also investment-broker talk and not baseball-card talk, so we've got no business talking it. Let's put this Dwight Evans rookie-card business in perspective. The Dwight Evans rookie card is just a baseball card, in a set of baseball cards where perspective and logic were sacrificed in favor of a shot of Luis Alvarado playing shortstop in a parking lot and making a throw to first up Mt. Kilamanjaro. The Dwight Evans card is in a set where the card of Joe Rudi shows three players equally, none of them being Joe Rudi. This is a set where one of the most attractive cards shows catcher Pat Corrales on his back, arms and legs in the air, screaming in agony. With cards like that in the set, the Dwight Evans card ought to outperform the set by 100 percent.

Let's put it this way: the Dwight Evans rookie card is a very good rookie card to have no matter what your reasons for having it may be. Is that better? You bet.

Paul's Score: 25

Kit's Score: 34

TOTAL SCORE: 59

1955 Bowman
Hank Aaron

61

And on the other hand there's Hank Aaron. Aaron has all the prerequisites for preeminent baseball stardom except two. Aaron was a wonderful hitter, arguably the best hitter in the best days of baseball. In a game where the home run is the feature attraction and singles and doubles are Looney Tunes, Aaron is at the top. Neither Babe Ruth nor Mickey Mantle nor Willie Mays has been able to surpass him. You can't call home runs a meaningful statistic all by its lonesome; all statistics are dependent on other statistics for their meaning. But Hammerin' Hank has enough numbers in the right places to be regarded as the best ever.

But he's not. Remember the three criteria for stardom? The three criteria for stardom (short version) are location, charisma and performance. Aaron had the performance but he never had the other two. He played in Atlanta and Milwaukee, a couple of swell cities but in there with Dubuque and Albuquerque as media hotbeds. Players could just go about their business and play in Atlanta and Milwaukee without the newspapers screaming "Hammerin' Hank Loses Head, Gets Nailed"; where's the fun in that?

And Aaron, for all his good, even-tempered qualities, never had charisma. When he flashed his winning smile and turned on the charm you were reminded of the macaroni and cheese you left on the stove. In his post-retirement appearances at card shows collectors have found him to be polite, quasi-personable and occasionally outgoing. Good, but not quite good enough.

The same applies to his 1955 Bowman card. It's a good card, though some people prefer the term "ugly as sin." They're referring to the Cheez Whiz color-TV border, but you have to realize at that time color TV was like microwave ovens and satellite dishes and VCRs all in one. A generation of Americans was in mortal danger of growing up believing that Milton Berle had gray hair, a gray face, gray funny teeth, and wore gray polka-dot dresses with snow on them, and color TV was going to deliver them truth and righteousness, and commercials. Bowman wanted to show it was in step with the times. If the times are now out of step with our times you can't blame the 1955 Bowman Hank Aaron.

Well, maybe you can. But it's only a $170 card (same as Willie Mays but less than Mickey Mantle and the high-numbered Ernie Banks), and it's Aaron's only appearance on a Bowman, save for some prototype '56 Bowmans that may or may not exist. Near Mint copies are hard to find because the color-TV cabinet nicks easily, but they're good buys; they've more than doubled their value in the last two years. And Topps' new Bowman line certainly won't hurt demand for old Bowmans, either.

Even if the baseball-card hobby doesn't always acknowledge stardom the way it should, it does place a premium on great play. In Hank Aaron's case, it's a big premium. And that's the way it ought to be.

Paul's Score: 22

Kit's Score: 37

TOTAL SCORE: 59

1957 Topps
Frank Robinson

Good old cheap old Topps. The company didn't use color photographs on its cards until 1957. Bowman had used full-color photographs on its cards four years earlier (and then quit, because it got too expensive). The innovative West Coast cardmakers at Mother's Cookies, bless their crumbly little heads, were using color photographs and slick finishes on their Pacific Coast League cards as early as 1952. Heck, even Esskay Hot Dogs was using color pictures of Baltimore Orioles on its weiner cards in 1954. But good old cheap old Topps couldn't find it in its pocketbook to use real color pictures, not the cheaper hand-tinted black-and-whites, until Bowman was swallowed whole and it was sure there were no other Bowmans on the horizon.

The 1957 set with those color pictures is something of a watershed set for Topps. There would be no more odd sizes after this and only one flirtation with a horizontal format. From 1957 on, cards would be a standard size and have standard features and carry some standard information on the backs. There would always be checklists, too, and most always team cards. Baseball cards are never truly boring, but a lot of the experimentation went out of baseball cards with the 1957 set. It was like old Mr. Firestone vulcanizing rubber on his kitchen stove. He probably *enjoyed* vulcanizing rubber over his kitchen stove, and would have preferred to fiddle with the sulfur and so forth over the burners forever, but he realized if he didn't get it out of the kitchen and into the factory, a.) his wife would leave him and b.) we'd all be driving around on Goodyear tires. Same with Topps.

Despite that, a lot of people love the 1957s, for some reason. They're a challenging set to complete in high grades, that's for sure. Perhaps because the printing process with the color photographs wasn't the best, many cards have a dull finish. Finding '57s with gloss usually involves calling in Indiana Jones. But even shiny '57s have a subdued, whipped look to them. It's a moody set, but it's nearly tripled in value in the last 14 months. Nice mood.

The '57 set, in keeping with its changing-of-the-guard look, is a big set for rookies. Three Hall of Famers and a couple of almost Hall of Famers debut in this set. Two of the three, Frank Robinson and Don Drysdale, appear early in the set, in the common low-number run, and are priced accordingly. The third, Brooks Robinson, appears in the scarcer mid-high-number run, and is not really priced accordingly.

The Frank Robinson card really isn't priced accordingly either, as long as it and Drysdale's card are priced equally. There was never an argument about Robinson's qualifications for the Hall of Fame. He hit 586 home runs in a stellar 21-year career, played on five World Series teams and is the only ballplayer to win Most Valuable Player awards in both leagues. He was the first black manager in the game, and seems to have found a home as skipper of his beloved Baltimore Orioles. Don Drysdale was none of those things, and was the subject of contentious debate when he and his 209–166 lifetime mark and his brush-'em-back temperament and his unbreakable scoreless-inning streak (since shattered by Orel Hershiser) were elected into the Hall of Fame. Maybe comparing pitchers and outfielders is like comparing apples and oranges. If that's the case, then Drysdale's a mighty puny, shriveled-up apple and Robinson's one grapefruit-sized son-of-a-citrus fruit. And there's no way that apple and that orange should be priced the same in the great farmer's market of life.

Looking at card values throughout the set—the Bill Mazeroski rookie at $20, the Whitey Herzog rookie at $18, the Rocky Colavito rookie at $35, Bobby Richardson at $90, the Jim Bunning rookie at $90—only the Drysdale rookie seems grievously overvalued and the Frank Robinson rookie grievously undervalued. Price movement on the Drysdale card has been quicker in the last year, too, and there's no good reason for it.

Frank Robinson has a look on his card like he's ready to spring at the world. He did that. Now if only his card could do the same thing.

Paul's Score:	22

Kit's Score:	37

TOTAL SCORE:	59

1955 Bowman
Al Barlick

63

Bowman's last year in the baseball-card business must really have been something. In its last-gasp push to dent Topps' bubble-gum armor, Bowman hauled out every screwball and knuckler and change-up in its arsenal—*and nothing worked.* Bowman put its player pictures inside honey-blonde Danish Delight television screens and filled the backs with personal recollections and even included cards of umpires, but to no avail. Topps was going to win, and Bowman was going to the rendering plant.

But maybe Bowman, ever the innovators right up to the end, was on to something with its umpire cards. T&M Sports, the company that today makes a successful line of umpire cards, would agree with that. Collectors agree with that; no umpire card is priced as a common, and Hall of Fame umpire cards bring more than many Hall of Fame player cards.

The names of many of the umpires aren't unfamiliar, either. Baseball fans of the 1950s and 1960s certainly haven't forgotten Hall of Famers Cal Hubbard and Jocko Conlan, and beer fans of the 1970s and 1980s recognize "nearsighted" Jim Honochick in an instant. But people remember Hank Soar and Nestor Chylak, Augie Donatelli, Tom Gorman and Frank Umont, too, and they remember Al Barlick.

There aren't really statistics for umpires, which tends to throw off the baseball fan's reasoning process somewhat. How many home runs did Al Barlick hit? None, but he called a ton and called back a few. How many runs did he score? None, but he rang up a bunch. How many runners did he throw out? Only the ones who said the magic word. Then how did he get into the Hall of Fame? By being square and honest and by callin' 'em as he was seein' 'em. Sure, there are a few criteria for great umpires—number of All-Star games and World Series worked— but essentially it's a matter of respect. And respect is a hard thing to quantify.

So why would you want an Al Barlick card, anyway? A couple of reasons. Barlick is in the Hall of Fame, and he isn't on any other card besides the '55 Bowman. His card is from a relatively tough high-number series. And it's reasonably priced. An Al Barlick card, adjusted for high-number inflation, costs half as much as a card of non-Hall of Famer Jim Honochick (the power of advertising! the power of beer! see Bob Uecker for details), and about as much as a card of Hank Bauer or Alvin Dark,

191

players who aren't Hall of Fame caliber and have plenty of cards. It's one of those cards that's a smart buy, and fun besides.

While we have a minute we're going to deliver a short euology for Bowman. Bowman made great baseball cards. It made cards that were too big and too small, and water-colored the daylights out of fuzzy old black-and-white photos, and it was great. While Bowman was in the card business to make money, it realized it wasn't selling Magna Cartas in wax packs five for a penny. Bowman didn't take the whole thing too seriously, and it wasn't afraid to try something different. Those are the best things you can say about any card company. Bowman was great.

Paul's Score: 24

Kit's Score: 35

TOTAL SCORE: 59

1948 Topps Magic
Ty Cobb

64

t took Topps a little while to get the hang of baseball cards. Contrary to popular perception, its first baseball set wasn't the brilliant 1952 set but something a little more pedestrian. Topps' first sets weren't the pedestrian 1951 Red Backs and Blue Backs, either, but something even more foot-powered. Its first effort was hardly an effort, even. The only reason they're called baseball cards is because some of them show baseball players. They're called Magic Photos, and they aren't really magic at all but disgusting. Topps would confuse magic and disgust several more times down through the years, but this was the first and probably the most disgusting time.

Topps Magic Photos are a 19-card subset of a 252-card set of actors, animals, personalities, boxers, bail bondsmen and fresh vegetables. It's more of a non-sport set than a sports or baseball set (like a later and slightly less strange Topps set, the 1952 Look 'N' See set), but it's hard to call the Magic Photos a set of cards because it's hard to call the photos cards. They're postage-stamp-size things, not very big and not very good-looking. They came with a blank front; a question on the back referred you to the wrapper for an answer. Since the question on the back and the wrapper on the front were all the fun you could have with the cards as long as the fronts stayed blank, you tended to follow directions with the Magic Photos. And the instructions told you how to "develop" the photos.

Here's the disgusting part. According to dealer Ted Koch, who remembers the Magic Photos for some reason, the directions told you to lick the wrapper and hold it on the card until a picture appeared. This was doable, except for one thing: The wrapper tasted terrible, so bad that rather than lick the wrappers most kids spit on them. It wasn't sanitary or nice, but the kids got a bang out of it, supposedly.

What kids got for their cent and their spit was a picture. You might get Cobb, Ruth or Gehrig, Jingles the Flying Goat, or Cleveland Indians 4–3 (the deciding game of the 1948 World Series). As far as excitement went, the set was definitely mixed.

The set is still mixed as far as grading goes. Because the cards are so small (7/8″ × 1½″) they're practically all corners. There's no such thing as original gloss with these, either, and since developing quality varied from card to card sometimes the black-and-white photo was clear and sometimes Cy Young's head drifted back into the shadows. Good high-grade examples were tough to find then and are even tougher today. If collectors wanted these cards they'd be expensive enough to make you gasp; as it is Cobb goes for about $200.

Despite the negatives with the cost and the kiddie-home-darkroom business there are some positives with the Magic Photos. The set shows primarily Hall of Famers when it's not showing Cleveland Indians newsreels. It has historical importance, too, when you look at where Topps was in 1948 and is now and realize it hasn't really gone anywhere; it just makes more money at it. And since Cobb wasn't in the 1951 Connie Mack All-Stars set and the others were, this makes the Magic Photos Cobb the only pre-1952 Topps Ty Cobb card.

Topps wasn't through with spit photos as a revenue center, unfortunately. Its 1956 Hocus Focus cards use the same high-tech method, with the same lousy results. From small things big days one day come; in Topps' case, it all started with spit.

Paul's Score: 33

Kit's Score: 26

TOTAL SCORE: 59

Studio Cabinet

65

The crowd was a little sparse on the front lawn the day the baseball-card photographer went to work, but he plied his young trade regardless. He took pictures of baseballers in poses resembling action from the game they played. Today they seem quaint, but in the 1880s those pictures, enlarged to cabinet size and reproduced, reflected the backyard nature of the game and supplied a strapping masculinity to parlors everywhere.

In 1887, and for about 20 years thereafter until the technology improved, the only card companies were photographic studios, and the only place where they could effectively shoot photographs of ballplayers were their studios. There was no spring training in Florida—nothing but beaches and alligators down there—no photo pits in the stadiums, no motor winders or 400-millimeter zoom lenses or rapid shutter speeds. So ballplayers did something unusual: They went to the photographers. The ballplayer and photographer collaborated on a conceit, on a blatantly fabricated photograph of a ballplayer fielding a perfectly stationary ball or making an immovable slide into a base tossed in the grass or laid on the floor, or making a grab for a line drive suspended from the ceiling by a string. The success or failure of their endeavor was irrelevant, because in those days reality could be suspended so much more easily. The stereopticon was a fantasy machine. The studio cabinets and Old Judges of the day were as real as they needed to be.

The photographs and the resulting cabinet cards were produced by a number of studios, Joseph Hall's Brooklyn studio being the most important. The studios apparently sent their baseball photographs to the card companies—Old Judge cigarettes, for instance—who sometimes used them for cards. So not all studio cabinets became cards, though all are interesting and desirable.

Baseball is history, like the songlines of the Australian bushmen, passed down from mothers and fathers to sons and daughters by a movement as easy and graceful as tossing a ball. Baseball is history in hardware, in the volumes of records you can bring back from microfilm and pore over. You can read every box score from every game Ty Cobb played in 1912, or read the story of Babe Ruth's 60th home run as they told it then and children read it then, the year the Titanic went down.

Baseball is social history, too. It's easy to read too much into baseball, but it always reflects the nature of the times. The men who played the game in the 19th century were tough because they had tough lives. They were the sons of immigrants, or immigrants themselves. Some had grown up in near wilderness. None were strangers to hard work from a young age. If they carried long knives it was only because many people did. If they drank and brawled it was because drinking and brawling was sport in those days. If there was inequality in baseball it was because there was inequality in life. You can't take baseball out of America and you can't take America out of baseball, and you get a feel for that in cards like these.

These cards are windows into a different era, and that makes them precious. Unfortunately, so does their scarcity. There's no definitive checklist of these cards because they're too scarce. Any value is based solely on what the seller is asking and the buyer is willing to pay. When and if you get the chance, become a buyer. These cards are history, and history never goes out of fashion.

Paul's Score: 35

Kit's Score: 24

TOTAL SCORE: 59

1956 Topps
Jackie Robinson

66

bout once a month *Baseball Cards* magazine gets a letter from a reader that goes something like this:

"Dear SCD [they haven't the foggiest idea who we are],

"Why isn't the last card of a ballplayer worth more money? A player's rookie card is worth money because it's the first card he's on, even though with all the minor-league cards it's not really his first card. So his last card ought to be worth just as much money as the first, because he isn't on any more cards than his last card. I am collecting all the last cards of my favorite stars and am buying them cheap because I know they will be worth lots of money someday. Please adjust your catalogs and price guides to reflect what I and lots of people around the country are doing. Sincerely, etc., etc."

About once a month *Baseball Cards* magazine throws out that letter, because BBC has heard it all before.

As we say time and time and time and time again, there's no accounting for collecting taste, and there shouldn't be. You want to collect the last cards of ballplayers, players' batting gloves, toothpicks, artificial limbs, tombstones? Fine. Just don't expect the rest of the collecting world to share your enthusiasm for what you do, and pay you lots of money when you decide you don't want to do it anymore.

The fact is that more collectors like collecting first cards than last cards because they can keep collecting a player's cards as the player develops—or doesn't develop, as the case may be. Last-card collectors have to collect at the end of the trail and after the fact. You get that last card and that's it. There's no last card coming again next year.

About the only time last-card collecting makes any sense is with some of the older players, such as Jackie Robinson. Robinson really didn't get a full crack at baseball cards. Bowman skipped him a couple of years, and his playing career was so short that even though Topps put him in every set except the '51s it seems like he was off baseball cards almost before he was on them.

And Robinson's departure was something quite a bit more than just the retirement of a great player. It was an acknowledgment that the job he had been brought in to do had been done, generally. Baseball's stars in 1956 included blacks such as Willie

Mays and Hank Aaron, and Puerto Ricans like Roberto Clemente and Minnie Minoso, and Venezuelans like Luis Aparicio. Their path to the big leagues was not easy, but was made easier by Jackie Robinson.

Jackie Robinson was tired by 1956, and ready to quit, but his card doesn't show that. His card doesn't show an ounce of quit. It shows instead a big, defiant smile. No, last-card collecting will never be where the money is. But in a few very special cases, it can be where the symbolism is. Jackie Robinson is one of those cases.

Paul's Score: 22

Kit's Score: 37

TOTAL SCORE: 59

1955 Topps
Yogi Berra

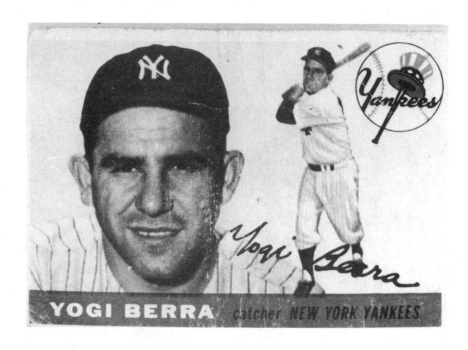

67

I t was a hot day, and Yogi Berra was dressed to the nines. Dressed to the nine-and-a-halfs for Yogi, if truth be told. Perforated shoes, Ban-Lon slacks, Munsingwear shirt, maybe some nice Interwoven socks in a pleasing alfalfa-field pattern, dandy Panama fedora. The works, according to the decidedly tacky tastes of Berra and the times. And Yogi's at a golf club, a nice golf club, a club that wouldn't even let Yogi play with the faucets if Yogi wasn't the greatest catcher on the greatest baseball team of the day.

Anyway, a lady—a pretty lady, a real Lana Turner type, dressed to the 10-and-a-halfs in something cottony and open-air—sees Yogi and recognizes him. Of course, how many guys that look like one-third of the Nairobi Trio are likely to be wandering around a fancy golf course dressed like a *Sports Illustrated* ad? The lady comes up to Yogi, introduces herself and says, "Gosh, Yogi, you sure look cool today."

Yogi sizes her up—she's about a size five—smiles at the complement and replies in kind, as only Yogi can, "Thanks, lady. You don't look too hot yourself."

That's how Yogi Berra is in danger of being remembered, as the "it ain't over 'til it's over" guy, as the malaprop movie reviewer, as the guy who remarked about Mickey Mantle's switchhitting, "The guy's naturally amphibious." It's not a bad reputation to carry through life, but in Berra's case it's an inaccurate one.

Berra was a superb offensive catcher—.285 lifetime hitter with 313 home runs—with few peers defensively. He was three times the American league's Most Valuable Player, and hit .322 with 124 RBI in 1950 and didn't win the award. He holds World Series records for most games and most hits, and he holds a baseball-card record you might not be aware of.

Berra appeared in the 1947 Tip Top bread set, and from then on, from 1948 until 1965, he appeared in every major set Topps and Bowman produced. Some players appeared in every Bowman set or put together a nice run in Topps, but no one else ever appeared in as many major sets of the 1940s, 1950s and early 1960s as Berra. Mantle got a late start in the Bowmans and missed some of the Topps issues; same with Mays. Warren Spahn missed the '54 and '55 Bowman sets. But Berra made them all, and is even in most of the popular food sets of his day, including the Post and Jell-O sets, the Drake's set and a

Wheaties set. He's even featured in one of the hard-to-find Viewmaster reels of the mid-1950s.

Unlike Stengel or Musial or Barlick or Ted Williams, Berra gives you a lot to choose from. His 1955 Topps card is as good a card as any to choose. Berra was coming off an MVP year in 1954, one in which he hit .307 with 22 home runs and 125 runs batted in, and he was heading to another MVP year in 1955, one in which he'd hit .272 with 27 dingers and 108 RBI. The card's a pretty one, with pleasant coloration and attractive shading, which is more than can be said for Berra. Because it's in a high-number series it's expensive—$225—but when you factor out the high-number inflation it's less expensive than the Banks and Kaline cards in the set, even though Berra ranks above Banks and Kaline in the baseball-card pecking order.

Pecking order, schmecking order. Yogi ordered a pizza once, and then was asked whether he wanted the pizza cut in four or eight slices. "Better make it four," he replied. "I don't think I can eat eight." Ah, Yogi. So much to love about the guy—especially when it comes to his baseball cards.

Paul's Score: 25

Kit's Score: 34

TOTAL SCORE: 59

1985 Topps
Mark McGwire

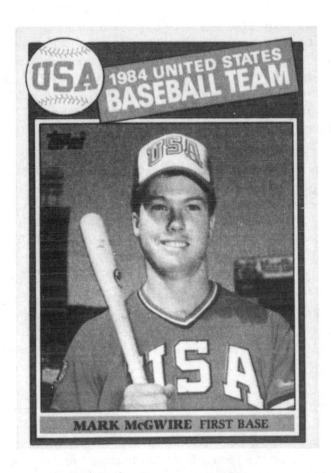

68

ven though, according to the creationist theory of baseball cards, rookie cards and update sets and everything had been formed out of the void in 1985 and people knew what they were doing and it was good, Topps (The Real One, The Creator) still wasn't entirely aware of what it was creating all the time. It's doubtful Topps knew just what it was up to in 1985 when it unleashed the U.S. Olympic Team subset on card consumers. And it's equally doubtful card consumers realized in 1985 just what Topps had unleashed on them. And that was good, too. But Topps created and collectors hesitated and after about two years you could still buy an Olympic subset for five or six bucks. The big cards were Cory Snyder and Oddibe McDowell, and they were all of $3.75 and $1.25. A Scott Bankhead card would have set you back 35 cents. Mike Dunne and Shane Mack cards were a dime apiece, and a Mark McGwire card—well, a card of first baseman/third baseman/pitcher Mark McGwire would have cost you a big, fat quarter. And that was real good.

It was real good only if you had bit the apple and realized that Mark McGwire cards would soon be $15, but then you would have realized your nakedness and been ashamed and been banished from the garden of baseball cards forever, and that's about all the mileage we're going to get out of that metaphor.

Once Mark McGwire started hitting home runs in 1987 you could hear his card go up in value. It was like hearing corn grow in the hot part of the summertime, like running over an opossum at midnight. It was $15 by the end of 1987. By the end of 1988 it was $15. It was $15 through 1989. It moved up to $18 to start the 1990s and it might be stuck there awhile.

It's a perplexing $18 card, though. You get a lot of questions for your $18 with this card. The first question is, "Is it a rookie card?" Technically, no. A rookie card is supposed to be the first card of a player in a regularly issued national set, *shown with a major-league team.* A rookie card of Dwight Gooden is supposed to show Gooden with the Mets, in a Mets uniform or a reasonable facsimile thereof. It's all right for a Juan Bell rookie card to show Bell in a Dodger uniform, even though he spent his rookie season with the Orioles. Airbrushes are acceptable, too. But Mark McGwire did not make his major-league debut for the U.S. Olympic Baseball Team. So the answer is, yes, it's McGwire's first card, but no, it's not his rookie card. It's the same as an update-set card, only not really.

The next question is, "Is this card going to be an $18 card forever?" No way.

The last question is, "Are you sure Topps didn't know what it was doing when it issued the '85 Mark McGwire Olympic card?" Nah. But in between it and the Roger Clemens and Kirby Puckett and Dwight Gooden true rookie cards languishing in the '85 set at $9–$10 each, and the Orel Hershiser rookie in there, too, the 1985 Topps set gives you a lot more to think about now at a set price of $90. Topps didn't create a monster in 1985. It created something better.

Paul's Score: 21

Kit's Score: 37

TOTAL SCORE: 58

1913 Fenway Breweries/ Tom Barker Baseball Honus Wagner

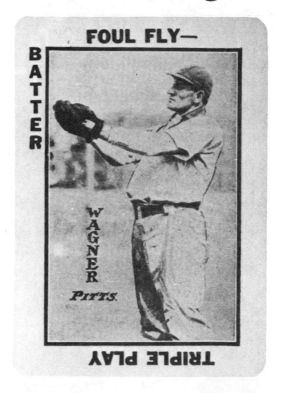

What is it? That's a question collectors often find themselves asking when confronted with old cards. Most of the time there's an answer. But often the answer isn't satisfactory. And sometimes the answer doesn't exist at all.

On Mar. 25, 1913, the Tom Barker Baseball Card Game was patented. As the Red Sox of that day were a powerhouse team led by Tris Speaker and Joe Wood, the Fenway Breweries of Boston made the game available at the "special price" of 50 cents—including their own Fenway Breweries insert card.

Who was Tom Barker? We're not really sure. And we don't know a lot about his set, either, other than it was a real game. There are hits, strikes, outs, and other logical baseball events on the cards. The backs look like playing-card backs, with the Tom Barker patent notice in something shaped strangely like a football.

While the cards are black and white, they have actual on-the-field photographs of almost every star of the era. A set with Honus Wagner, Ty Cobb, Joe Jackson, Cy Young, Wahoo Sam Crawford, Christy Mathewson, Walter Johnson, Rube Marquard, Grover Cleveland Alexander, John McGraw, Joe Tinker, Johnny Evers and Frank Chance has to be attractive, even if we don't know much about it.

In addition to the portraits and action shots of the stars (which appear to have been taken on the sidelines during pregame warmups), there are some legitimate action shots. Dust flies, the crowd blurs and the umpire becomes a blob, and the players in the pictures go unidentified.

The set has some other unanswered questions. On the Home Run Baker card there's a stamped advertisement for Fenway, "The Beer Without a Substitute." Whether this stamping was made on all Bakers in the Fenway set, or all Bakers in all Tom Barker sets, or just on the Baker in this one set, is anyone's guess.

And just what is Honus Wagner doing on his card? Maybe the ball has just landed in his glove. If not, he sure trusts his judgment; he's not looking skyward, that's for sure. He appears to be engaged in some sort of ritual, not playing baseball. But, hey, he's in the Hall of Fame and so he's entitled to do whatever makes sense for him at the time.

Prices for sets and individual cards are based on whatever the seller wants and the buyer is willing to pay. They have to be. Some have catalog values and some don't, and sometimes the catalog value is just an arbitrary number. But cards and sets such as these are available if you seek them out. And as long as they make you happy, you'll do well with them.

Paul's Score: 32

Kit's Score: 26

TOTAL SCORE: 58

1958 Topps
Mickey Mantle
All-Star

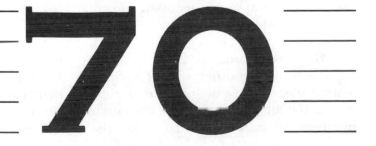

There have been at least 10 articles in hobby periodicals in the last two years speculating why all-star cards aren't worth more money. The authors all compare the price of a player's regular card to his all-star card and conclude the all-star card is undervalued, and due for a rise, and a real bargain, and every single one of them miss the point.

The point is: all-star cards aren't worth money because people don't want them, and will never be worth that much money because collectors will never want them as badly as a player's regular card.

Now, to explain what an all-star card is, and why it's worthless. Beginning in 1958, and continuing in a more-or-less regular fashion, Topps has issued a special subset each year recognizing an all-star team. The all-star team is usually the previous season's all-star team, though that isn't always the case and isn't always stated. And sometimes the all-star team has a sanctioning body—*Sport* magazine or *The Sporting News*—and sometimes it's just Topps' picks. Sometimes the all-stars chosen are only the all-stars Topps can show (Ted Williams and Stan Musial were left off of a couple of teams that way).

All-star cards are usually saddled with several tons of geegaws and shields and eagles and diamonds, and usually the backs are surpassed as interesting reading only by toothpaste instructions. In a couple of cases the backs are nothing but puzzle pieces.

That's what we mean by worthless. Puzzle pieces? If you're going to put a puzzle piece on the back of a baseball card you might as well write in big block letters on the back, "THIS CARD IS WORTHLESS! STICK IT IN YOUR BICYCLE SPOKES! LET YOUR DOG PLAY WITH IT!" Donruss knew enough to separate its puzzle pieces and its cards, and its puzzle pieces are still worthless. Topps put puzzle pieces on the backs of all-star cards, and now no one wants to buy all-star cards except some magazine writers in dirty trenchcoats who keep nudging people and saying, "You wanna see something big?", and then haul out a '58 Topps Mantle all-star.

"It's the most affordable Mantle card of the 1950s," they tell the cops, which is another way of saying it's the cheapest. The Mantle all-star is in a high-number series, but that year for some reason the high numbers were the common series and the low numbers are scarce, and that makes the Mantle all-star card a low-demand item from a common series. Not exactly the ideal combination if rapid appreciation is your goal.

But wait just a minute here. The card was a $12 item two years ago. It's $50 now. If you had bought 20 of the Mantle all-stars then and held onto them, that's $760 in paper profits on a $240 paper investment. Not too darn bad.

The Mantle all-star remains the least expensive Mantle card of a decade full of expensive Mantle cards. That fact alone doesn't make it a buy, and the fact that it's a silly card doesn't automatically make it a no-buy. It just makes it interesting.

Paul's Score: 26

Kit's Score: 31

TOTAL SCORE: 57

1988 Minnesota Twins Team-Issue Kirby Puckett

71

ajor League Baseball can sometimes be a royal pain in the patoot, if you know what we mean. Oh, sure, they do run America's Game, the Pastime, and they do do things like make commercials with Jack Morris and Tommy Lasorda and Mark McGwire, but mostly they exist to give the commissioner's office a real live office and to make life miserable for all these unscrupulous fly-by-night operations who try to issue unauthorized pirate card sets without MLB's permission.

Like the Minnesota Twins, for instance.

Uh-huh. The Twinkies. Homerdome denizens, 1987 World Champions, card piraters.

It happened like this. The Twins have been making a postcard set for several years. Many teams make postcard sets, or at least postcards that its players can use for autograph requests. The Twins' postcards are particularly nice, full-color cards showing the players in all the classic poses.

In 1983 the Twins began producing a card set to accompany the postcard set. The card set was sold at concession stands and through the mail, and was a success, even if it did show one of the worst teams ever in baseball. Not such a success that the Twins felt compelled to go nationwide with the thing, but a small-scale, regional success. The Twins issued card sets every year from 1983 through 1987.

In 1988 the Twins were excited about everything, including their card set. The team had won the World Series the year before, and so the card set had a small gold embossed crown surrounded by the legend "1987 World Champions" in the right-hand corner. The sets were issued early in the 1988 season, and sales were moderately brisk. Then Major League Baseball told the Twins they had to stop selling the card sets because they weren't licensed by Major League Baseball to show the Twins' logo.

The Twins didn't have permission to show their own logo on their own card set, in other words.

The edict was passed down with the force of Nazi Germany on a good day. The Twins were given two choices: either stop selling the sets and destroy all leftovers, or stop selling the sets, start giving them away, and deface the backs to indicate you're

215

sorry, you're stupid, and it will never happen again, master. The Twins chose the first route.

As a result, there are fewer than 2,000 1988 World Champions Twins sets in existence. The cards look great, show all the Twins stars—which right now consist of Kirby Puckett and Frank Viola—and are tremendously undervalued considering their scarcity. The set catalogs for $8; if you find any at that price, buy them all. Forty dollars is a more realistic price, and even that's cheap considering the numbers out there.

The '88 Twins team set is one of the great secret sets in a hobby where there are supposed to be no secrets. Kirby Puckett is the best player in the set. Go get it.

Paul's Score: 22

Kit's Score: 35

TOTAL SCORE: 57

1987 Topps
Will Clark

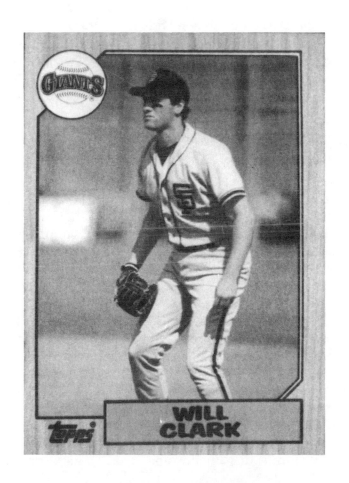

72

The best buy among 1980s sets has to be the 1987 Topps set. There's an astounding collection of rookies in the set. Bo Jackson, Bobby Bonilla, Randy Myers, Mike Greenwell, Ruben Sierra, Mitch Williams, Mark McGwire, Pete Incaviglia, Rafael Palmiero, Devon White, Barry Larkin, Kevin Mitchell, Glenn Braggs, and Will Clark all have rookie cards in the 1987 Topps set, but the set catalogs for $35 and sells in the $30–$35 range. You can still pick one up very cheaply at shows. With the '87 Donruss set with fewer rookies at $65 and the '87 Fleer set with fewer rookies too (but with Kevin Seitzer) at $90, the Topps set is undervalued by about 50 percent. Sure, a lot of '87 Topps sets are out there; 1987 was the last year Fleer and Donruss really underproduced compared to Topps, so '87 Fleer and Donruss are sort of scarce. But there are more '88 Donruss and Fleer sets than '87 Topps sets, and both those sets—with fewer key rookies—sell for more than the '87 Topps set.

You really have your choice of rookies in the '87 set. Barry Larkin is developing into a top-flight N.L. shortstop, and a real offensive threat. Rafael Palmiero is going to be a .300-plus hitter for most of the next decade. Greenwell and Sierra are going to be the Billy Williamses and Willie Stargells of their time. Devon White has the potential to be the first redefining outfielder since Paul Blair, and he'll be an exceptional hitter. Every one of these cards except for Greenwell sell in the $1–$3 range—for the time being.

And then there's Will Clark. Clark hit a home run in his first major-league plate appearance, and just kept going from there. He's brash, he's funny, and he can hit every way you want. You want power? Clark can smash 'em with the best. You want average? Clark can go over .300 the way most hitters go over .250. Clark plays in a popular media market and has great fan rapport. His rookie card in the '87 Topps set sells for $5, which is $30 less than the same card in the Fleer set, and up $3 over the last six months. It's a handsome card of a handsome young talent.

This card has everything going for it. It's a good card from a good-looking set. It's a Topps card, so it'll always have a ready market somewhere. It shows a hitter who's been productive on a consistently high level over his first three seasons. It's relatively inexpensive, but promises not to be inexpensive for long. Anything else? Oh, yeah: It's great fun at parties. Get this one.

Paul's Score: 23

Kit's Score: 34

TOTAL SCORE: 57

1963 Fleer
Maury Wills

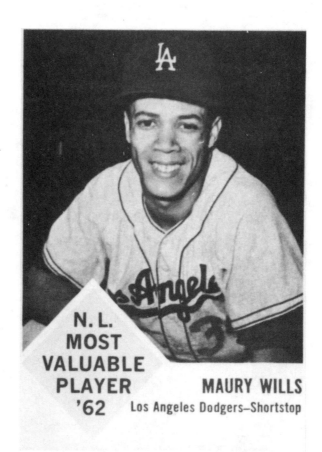

73

For a time in the early 1960s Fleer was convinced it was going to be the cardmaker for all seasons. It made a basketball set in 1960. It was a nice basketball set, and it did a real nice job of acquainting Fleer with the First Law of Basketball Cards, which Topps had learned all about when it made a basketball-card set two years earlier: the reason there aren't more basketball cards is because nobody buys basketball cards. It made football sets. Fleer's 1960 American Football League set is the Don Mossi of football-card sets. The only way these cards could be homelier was if they were painted on black velvet. Fleer got out of the football-card business after three years, a victim of the Second Law of Football Cards: if you don't make a lot of football cards, people won't buy a lot of football cards.

And Fleer made baseball cards, too. In 1959 it signed an exclusive contract with Ted Williams and issued an 80-card set of nothing but Ted Williams cards. Nice set, too, if you like Teddy Ballgame cards. The next two years, Fleer issued sets of Baseball Greats. The sets were unattractive and meaningless, and featured a factory-applied ultra-dull, anti-gloss finish. These are the only baseball cards ever where the backs are glossier than the fronts. Taken together, the three sets taught Fleer all about the Third and Fourth Laws of Baseball Cards: if you make a set of only one player, people will buy it like there's only one card in the set; and if people wanted a Johnny Kling card, they would have bought it when they still knew who Johnny Kling was.

Finally in 1963 Fleer did what Fleer should have done in 1959 and challenged Topps directly with a baseball-card set. Considering the cards could have looked like the 1960 AFL football set, they didn't turn out half bad. They're only a little dull, and there is one card in the set that's at least a little interesting.

Maury Wills was coming off an MVP year in 1962. He hit .299, stole 104 bases and led the Dodgers to a World Series win over the Yankees. But in a throwback to the old Topps vs. Bowman days, Wills wasn't in the 1963 Topps set, and wouldn't be until 1967; however, he was in the 1963 Fleer set.

There are plenty of stars in the '63 Fleer set—Clemente, Mays, Koufax, Yastrzemski, Spahn, Drysdale, Bob Gibson—and there are even a couple of scarcities—Joe Adcock and the checklist. If you're looking to buy scarce cards out of this set that are priced at levels way below their scarcity, those are the cards to go after. Actually, the entire set is relatively affordable. The Wills card has almost doubled in value over the last couple of years, and it's still only $25.

Naturally, if Wills had been able to build on his MVP year of 1962 the '63 Fleer would be a dynamite card. But as it is, it's still pretty powerful.

Fleer was able to issue 63 baseball cards in 1963. After that, Topps took Fleer to court and blocked Fleer from producing the rest of its 1963 set. Fleer got out of the football-card business after that year, too. It would be another 18 years before we would have another Fleer baseball card to kick around.

Paul's Score: 23

Kit's Score: 33

TOTAL SCORE: 56

1978 Topps
Paul Molitor/
Alan Trammell

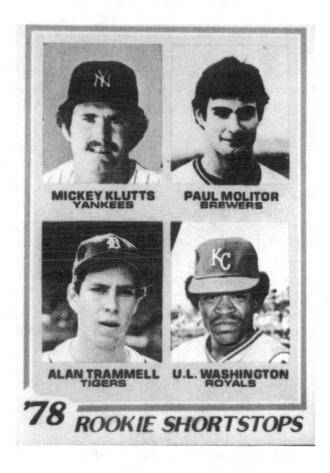

MICKEY KLUTTS
YANKEES

PAUL MOLITOR
BREWERS

ALAN TRAMMELL
TIGERS

U.L. WASHINGTON
ROYALS

'78 ROOKIE SHORTSTOPS

74

I f sometimes it seems as though everyone's a prospective Hall of Famer, that's because everyone is a prospective Hall of Famer. Tony Oliva is a prospective Hall of Famer. Marty Marion is a prospective Hall of Famer. Jim Kaat, Ferguson Jenkins, Rollie Fingers, Jim Palmer, and Tommy John are all prospective Hall of Famers. Jack Clark is a prospective Hall of Famer. Alfredo Griffin is a prospective Hall of Famer, though he will have to pick up the pace somewhat. If a ballplayer is good enough to make it into the major leagues, theoretically he ought to be good enough to make it into the Hall of Fame. Heck, Rabbit Maranville made it. Candy Cummings made it. Candy Cummings won 21 games in the National League, but was elected to the Hall of Fame because he supposedly invented the curveball. They don't know for sure he invented the curveball; they just give him credit for it. Heck, Rip Sewell won 143 games in the National League, and invented the eephus for sure, and he's not in the Hall of Fame. You figure.

By those standards Paul Molitor and Alan Trammell are prospective Hall of Famers. But by most tough standards Molitor and Trammell are Hall of Fame caliber. Molitor holds a World Series record for most hits in a game and has one of the longest contemporary hitting streaks. His career average is .299, he's pushing 2,000 career hits, he has 317 career stolen bases, and he shows no sign of slowing down or giving in to anything but the usual string of debilitating injuries his flesh is heir to. He's led the league in runs scored twice and doubles once, and played with fire throughout. Molitor's game is an all-over game, like Andre Dawson's, and he's done it just about as well as it can be done for the last 12 seasons.

Trammell's game is more defined because his position hasn't varied, but the numbers are comparable to Molitor's: .290 career average, 1,600 hits, 133 home runs, speed, and state-of-the-art defense. Both players seem unusually injury-prone, but both play like Richard the Lion-Hearted when they're healthy.

Their rookie cards are the same card, as you might have guessed. Both players appear on the Rookie Shortstops card along with the unfortunately named Mickey Klutts and the unfortunately toothpicked U.L. Washington (whose major shortcoming as a hitter was that he kept confusing his bat with his toothpick, and took too many unnecessary shots in the face for the team. As you might have suspected, he also had trouble getting around on the fastball). The Molitor-Klutts-Trammell-Washington card carries a $40 value in Near Mint, which is not bad at all when you consider the Dawson card sitting back in the previous year's set at $35, and the Rookie Catchers card in the '78 set with the rookie cards of no-chance Hall of Famers Ernie Whitt, Lance Parrish, and Bo Diaz, and the pantomime rookie card of Dale Murphy at $25. In fact, by those standards, the Molitor-Trammell card is a great buy, perhaps the best buy in late-1970s rookie cards. Any rookie card showing two popular players who have put up 12 years' worth of Hall of Fame–quality numbers has to have a lot of room to grow beyond the $40 level.

This is an ugly card with attractive possibilities. That's usually the way it is. But in this case you ought to be able to live with it.

Paul's Score: 23

Kit's Score: 33

TOTAL SCORE: 56

1966 Topps
Willie McCovey

75

T his is the part of the book where we talk about high numbers and cards in series.

As grown-ups, we say we used to love cards issued in series. As kids, we felt a little differently about it.

The idea for cards in series came from Bowman and was copied by Topps. Collectors had nothing to do with it.

The premise behind cards in series was that if you only had a 132-card set, and you put out all 132 cards at once, kids would buy packs of cards only until they got the 132 cards. Then they'd put their money into annuities or licorice whips or something.

On the other hand, if a card/gum company split that 132-card set into two 66-card sets, and maybe short-printed 16 or 20 cards, kids would have to buy just about as many gum packs to get those 66 cards as they did to get the 132 cards, and then they'd have to start all over. Double your pleasure, double your fun.

This idea worked all right when there were only two or three series of cards. But when there got to be seven and eight series of cards things got a little out of whack.

The first series would be issued around March or April, and would usually hang around until May—though if you went to the right senile corner grocery store you could be buying first-series cards into August. The second series would be on sale from May through the middle of June. The third series would run into July. The fourth series would run through August. And then the fifth, sixth, seventh and eighth series would show up for two weeks in September. You never knew when you bought a pack of baseball cards in the fall whether you'd get number 200 or number 600. Sure, the packs said "New Series!!", but *which* new series?

Yeah. We used to love cards in series. The only reason we love cards in series now is because it makes some sets worth $2,000 more than the set from the previous year, and makes all commons worth $15. And we don't have the sets or the commons anyway.

One of the toughest high-number series to complete is the last series of 1966 cards. Not only is the series scarce in general, but there are about 20 cards in the series that were single-printed, which makes them about half again as scarce as the scarce commons in this series. And some of them are team pictures and some of them are stars and some of them are Hall of Famers. And one of them is Willie McCovey.

McCovey is another one of those ballplayers that everyone knew belonged in the Hall of Fame but no one was sure why. He hit 521 home runs, hit .270 for his career, and had a run of eight years where he hit 31 or more home runs seven times. He was Rookie of the Year and MVP, and still holds the National League record for grand slams.

His 1966 card is buried up in the 523–598 high-number series. Worse yet, it's a short-print. What that means is your chances of finding this card are about as great as your chances of bringing peace to the Middle East. It also means if you find this card in acceptable shape, you should buy it.

The card catalogs at $95, but it's tougher than that. It's as tough as card #598, Gaylord Perry, which catalogs at $250 because of its last-card-in-the-set position. The McCovey card has gone from $48 to $95 in the last two-plus years, and it will keep going as long as collectors keep realizing the true scarcity of 1966 high numbers.

It's been said before but needs to be said again: You can't go wrong with high-number cards of Hall of Famers. Willie Mc-Covey in particular.

Paul's Score: 24

Kit's Score: 32

TOTAL SCORE: 56

1983 Topps Update
Darryl Strawberry

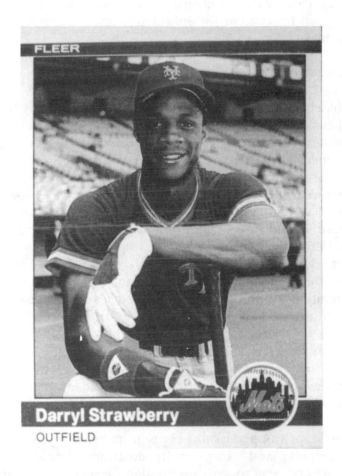

Darryl Strawberry
OUTFIELD

76

If there was such a thing as a baseball-card historian, he would be tempted to say that baseball cards experienced a realignment in 1984, and he'd probably expect a Pulitzer Prize for it. Before 1984, he'd say, baseball cards were just baseball cards. They came in packs with gum, and you chewed the gum when you opened the pack and stuck the cards in your back pocket and pinned the triples and quadruples to your bicycle spokes, and built card houses with them, and that was the state of the baseball-card market prior to 1984. After 1984, he'd continue, baseball cards were an investment, a spectacular way to make money, an instrument for speculation wilder than a common stock in 1928.

Wrong. Wrong on all counts.

The baseball-card market didn't change the instant Baby New Year 1984 came sliding down the pole. The fundamental change in the baseball-card market in 1984 was the product of several incremental changes in the market made over the previous two or three years. The introduction of competition in 1981 improved the market tremendously. Compare a 1980 Topps set to a 1984 or '85 model if you don't believe it. Look at the innovations introduced by Donruss and Fleer—Action All-Stars, Diamond Kings, Hall of Fame Heroes, Star Stickers—and the responses by Topps—scratch-offs, foldouts, all-star glossy send-in sets. And whatever you do when you write your baseball-card history, don't forget about the contributions of pre-1984 Topps Traded sets on the explosion of the card market in 1984.

The Traded set is another reaction to competition, but in a roundabout sort of way. When Topps issued cards in series it had its last series of the year to catch late trades and hot rookies. If a player changed teams or was promoted from the minors, Topps could simply slip him into the seventh or eighth series. When Topps stopped issuing cards in series, except for a couple of unpopular and exceptionally unattractive traded subsets, there was no way to get those traded players into the set with their right teams and in their right uniforms. And since Topps had no pressure to get its cards on the market in January or before, there was no pressure to catch any trades or show any hot rookies. Competition forced Topps to get its cards out earlier, and come up with some way of catching trades and showing rookies. Its solution was a boxed, end-of-year set sold as a complete set—no wax packs—showing traded players and rookies. The Traded set.

Topps issued its first Traded set in 1981. There have been better traded sets since; the highlight of the 1981 set was Tim Raines' first card.

(Curious thing about traded/update sets: rookies have more popular and valuable cards than traded players, but the cards of rookies aren't technically rookie cards. They're first cards, and the first card of a rookie in a nationally distributed wax-pack set is that player's rookie card. But people buy those first cards like they're rookie cards anyway, so it's all just jargon.)

The 1983 set was much better, because it has Darryl Strawberry's first card. This card is the prototypical valuable card, traded set or not: the first card of an outfielder who plays in New York and hits home runs. Never mind that Strawberry is far from a complete ballplayer; he has the qualities card buyers want in a baseball card, and his card will continue to outpace the rest of the baseball-card market as long as Strawberry stays in New York and has reasonably productive seasons.

Is it right for Strawberry's card to sell for $60? No. But right has nothing to do with it.

Paul's Score: 26

Kit's Score: 30

TOTAL SCORE: 56

1974 Topps
Willie McCovey
(Washington)

WASHINGTON   1st BASE

WILLIE McCOVEY   "NAT'L LEA."

77

The 1974 Topps set is really a piece of work. Not quite the piece of work the '73 set is, but a good chunk of union labor nonetheless. There are not quite as many cards of ballplayers hidden behind umpires, or cards of eight ballplayers converging on a fly ball where you have to figure which player is the player named on the card, but it does have a card of Steve Garvey that one of the writers for *Baseball Cards* magazine praised for its impressionistic qualities but which is really just a fuzzy photo. It also has a card of Jesus Alou without a position listed and a shining single card that unites the brave, dashing Four Musketeers of 1970 pitching: Dave Freisleben, Ron Diorio, Frank Riccelli and Greg Shanahan. Just on the remote possibility that you didn't realize this, the brave, dashing four combined won 37 games and lost 63 games lifetime. Thirty-four of the wins and 60 of the losses came from Freisleben. And this card is not even the cheapest rookie card in the set. That honor goes to the Rookie Pitchers card which shows Craig Swan, Rick Henninger, Glenn Abbott and Dan Vossler. Next time you start thinking all rookie cards are automatically worth scads of money, let us take you shopping in the 1974 Topps set.

The 1974 Topps set is also the first set to be issued as a complete set, without series. No more late-in-the-year surprises, which were usually along the lines of a new George Korince rookie card or distribution that ended somewhere east of Portland. Maine, that is.

Even with all the fun rookie cards in the '74 Topps set (and how about the one with Leo Foster, Tom Heintzelman, Dave Rosello, and Frank Taveras? Huh?), the real reason this set's a piece of work has to do with the San Diego Padres—or, as the '74 set refers to them, "Washington Nat'l Lea."

Rumors of franchise shifts are nothing new. The Chicago White Sox have moved to Tampa/St. Petersburg at least five times since 1987. The Seattle Mariners have pulled up stakes for Denver about as many times. But the card companies don't believe any of this franchise-shift talk. If they did, with the long lead times they produce under these days, they'd have the Chisox in Florida and the Mariners in Washington, D.C., every year.

However, when the San Diego Padres were sold in 1973, and the new owners promised to move the club to Washington as soon as Major League Baseball approved, Topps took the bait whole. Major League Baseball would approve; that was just a formality. The Padres were headed east for sure.

But it never happened. Ray Kroc, who made a billion serving up a billion billion hamburgers at a million billion McDonald's restaurants, bought the team and pledged to keep it in San Diego as long as he could get on the p.a. system every now and then and rip his own players, and the umpires, and the food in the stands. The other owners approved without hesitation, and the Padres never left.

Ah, but they did on those Topps cards. Fifteen different cards were printed with the "Washington Nat'l Lea." team ID before the presses could be stopped and the error corrected. Unfortunately, San Diego then made San Diego now look like the Big Red Machine; most of the players with error cards are all-time greats like Vincente Romo, Rich Troesdon, Rich Morales and Dave Hilton. Their "Washington Nat'l Lea." cards are $3.75–$4, and interesting; that's about it. The Willie McCovey card is a different story. It's a $20 card, and scarcer than its price indicates. With its nachos-and-mustard airbrush job, it's also one of the strangest cards you can buy out of a regular-run Topps set. That oddity factor combined with McCovey's Hall of Fame status will keep the card from ever going down. And as for going up, it's a piece of work. Pieces of work very rarely come down.

Paul's Score: 24

Kit's Score: 32

TOTAL SCORE: 56

1989 Upper Deck
Dale Murphy

Dale Murphy

fter seeing how the Big One became the Big Three and finally the Big Four, a company called Upper Deck made it five big baseball-card companies in 1989. Upper Deck has had some interesting people involved in its operation: a foreign-born printing whiz who at first didn't know a baseball card from a get-well card, a couple of former card dealers, some former grocery executives, one of the major stockholders in the company that makes Lionel trains, and two baseball players—Wally Joyner and Dwayne Buice. The baseball players were forced out by the Major League Baseball Players' Association halfway through the licensing process, one of the card dealers left and was replaced by another card dealer, the Lionel-train guy supplied money when the company needed it, and the whole thing kept chugging along.

Upper Deck's gimmick, if you want to call it that, is that it makes a high-end card. Sort of the Gucci bag of cards. Upper Deck claims superior photo quality and undingable corners and anti-counterfeiting holograms and absolute random collation, but an Upper Deck card doesn't have anything substantial that couldn't be found some other 1989 card. They're not even scarce in a relative sense; according to calculations, about 1.3 million of each Upper Deck card was printed.

But Upper Deck has been very successful in creating the illusion of scarcity and desirability. It said, "We suggest that our cards sell for 89 cents a pack"—double what everyone else's cards are supposed to sell for—but it didn't raise a ruckus when its cards sold for $1.50 and $2 a pack. It didn't holler that it was unfair to kids when Ken Griffey, Jr. Upper Deck cards began selling for $7.50 and $10 and $12 each. Upper Deck was the first card company to enter the card business with a marketing plan more sophisticated than, "Let's sell as many cards as we can to as many people as we can at every store everywhere." Upper Deck's plan—"If we price it out of the range of most people, most people will simply readjust their range"—isn't a particularly nice plan, but it works; give them credit for that.

And give Upper Deck credit for inadvertently slipping a major error into its first set. About 20,000 cards into the press run someone noticed that Dale Murphy's card was printed with the negative reversed—with everything backwards, in other words. It's difficult to spot, since Murphy's arms cover most of the lettering, and the "A" on the cap looks just about the same backwards and forwards. The presses were stopped and the error corrected, but the cards that had already been printed and packaged were sent out. Early wax boxes and foil packs contained the error cards.

Like the Bonds/Ray Donruss error, the Murphy error is a known quantity. The company announced how many exist. Because of that, we can make a real determination on whether or not it's worth it. The card currently sells for around $150. Part of that is the pure error; part of that is the fact that it's an error card of Dale Murphy. Murphy's a popular player, but generally an overvalued one. That makes his error card a little overvalued, too.

The Bonds/Ray error is scarcer and more significant than the Murphy error and a better buy if you can find it. But if you can't find it, the Murphy error ought to outperform the market by about 10 percent over the next year, and by more beyond that.

Upper Deck made other errors in its first set, but none more important than the Murphy error. Even the high end makes mistakes.

Paul's Score: 22

Kit's Score: 34

TOTAL SCORE: 56

R-312
Vaughan/Wagner

Floyd Vaughan, present Pirate Short Stop, and Coach Hans Wagner, who was one of the game's greatest.

79

ere's a fine young lad," Arthur Godfrey used to say when he was closing out his titanic television and radio career by doing commercials for Colgate toothpaste. "But what about his teeth?"

Well, you can ask the same question about the R-312 Vaughan/Wagner card, and you don't have to play the ukelele or kick Julius LaRosa off the set to do it. Here's a fine-looking card. But what the heck is it?

It's an R-312, but that's admittedly not much help. It's an R-312 of a Hall of Famer teaching another Hall of Famer the fine art of throwing a ball on the ground, and that's not much more help. But that's just about all the help we can give you.

We can tell you something definite about the people pictured, though. Honus Wagner was the greatest shortstop ever, Ozzie Smith and John Henry Lloyd included. He played for 20 years, hit .329 for his career and stroked 3,430 hits. Arky Vaughan was the second-best shortstop Pittsburgh ever had, and probably the second-best hitting shortstop ever, next to Wagner. He was a crackerjack fielder like Wagner, and like Honus, he was a man of undisputed character. Vaughan was elected to Cooperstown in 1985.

Now, back to the card. The R-312s were produced in 1936. They're black-and-white photos tinted in pastels, like many contemporary postcards. There are 50 cards known in the set, 25 individual player cards, 14 multiplayer photos—many of which feature one or more Hall of Famers—and 11 action shots. The R-312s were given out as a premium, and maybe because of that they're large and fragile. They're very scarce, but since they're seldom cataloged few collectors besides the specialists know just how rare they are.

And that's the problem with these cards. It's hard to imagine better cards coming out of the year 1936. Compare these to the late-period Goudeys, the four-in-ones and the premiums, and see which ones you like best. Figure in the percentage of Hall of Famers and the fact that two cards—the Vaughan-Wagner and a Lefty Grove–Connie Mack card—show two HOFers each and the R-312s seem tremendous.

They do, don't they? But they're not; not really. You have to know what you're buying when you buy these, but there's always a good chance you might be buying them from a dealer who doesn't know what he's dealing. Take advantage of these cards if you can; enjoy them at any rate.

Paul's Score: 28

Kit's Score: 28

TOTAL SCORE: 56

1988 Topps Traded
Jim Abbott

80

When it comes to making money by manipulating collectors' likes and wants, Topps is Svengali, the undisputed viceroy of the ashpile, the Big Limburger. No one has as many ways to extract money from collectors, and no one is as good at making collectors fly into the flame for an issue. For instance, in 1989 a collector who collects Topps has to have the regular Topps set for the No. 1 draft-pick cards; the '89 Big set because it has the only '89 cards of the '88 Olympic team, and the first Topps cards of Jack Clark in his proper new uniform, and the first Topps cards of Junior Felix and Jerome Walton; the Topps Doubleheaders because they're supposedly a test issue and supposedly very few were made (though throughout the summer you could walk down to the neighborhood metroplex liquor store and, once you blew the inch and a half of dust off of the box, buy as many Doubleheaders as you wanted); the Topps glossy rookies because they're rookies; a Topps Bowman set because it has different rookies from all the other sets that show rookies; a Topps Tiffany (glossy) set because 2.8 million weren't made; and a Topps Traded set for the second cards of all the players who had their first cards in the Topps Big set.

It was that way in 1988, too. You had to have the Big cards because they were a new and supposedly limited edition (they weren't), and the Topps U.K. American Baseball set because it was theoretically available only Over There (when in reality it was available only Over Here), and you had to have the 1988 Traded set because it had cards of the 1988 U.S. Olympic Baseball team.

Topps had learned a lesson with Mark McGwire and the 1984 Olympic baseball team. Topps knew that collectors knew what happened with the 1984 Olympic-team cards, and Topps knew that collectors knew that if they bought the heck out of whatever set had 1988 Olympic-team cards, one or two of those cards would do what Mark McGwire's Olympic card did, and we all know what that was. So Topps put the Olympic-team cards in one of its most vulnerable sets, the 1988 Traded set. And collectors bought the heck out of them. And collectors drove up the prices of the sets. How far? A Fleer Update set is $12. A Donruss Rookies set is $10. A Topps Traded set is $20.

Never mind the rookies with this set; the key cards are the Olympic cards. Robin Ventura, a hitting machine in the Wade Boggs mold, is good. Ty Griffin, a second baseman who may give Ryne Sandberg a run for his money with the Cubs, is good.

Flamethrower Andy Benes is good. Ed Sprague is good. But the best of them all is Jim Abbott.

Jim Abbott is good because he has only one hand, and is pitching in the major leagues in spite of it. Baseball-card buyers might admire his courage but they also want to see his stump. They want to see him field bunts and spear comebackers through the box.

It's not very nice, but it does do nice things for the value of his cards. And the longer Jim Abbott stays in the majors the more good things it will do for his cards. The 1988 Topps Traded set is a good buy, even at its stiff price. Abbott is a big part of the reason why. But he isn't the entire reason why.

Paul's Score: 26

Kit's Score: 28

TOTAL SCORE: 54

1967 Topps
Rod Carew

A. LEAGUE ROOKIE STARS

ROD CAREW • 2B
MINNESOTA TWINS

HANK ALLEN • OF
WASHINGTON SENATORS

81

I t gets awfully tiresome writing and talking about rookie cards all the time, but in the postwar card world that's what all the fuss is about. So here we go again.

There are two big rookie cards in the 1967 Topps set you ought to be concerned with. The one you're probably a little more familiar with shows Tom Seaver. It's a $750 card that was a $250 card a couple of years ago. It is in a high-number series, and it does show a future Hall of Famer, so it is desirable simply for that, but it has a limited horizon. Where's a $750 card going to go without being recognized? $800? $1,000?

The other big rookie card in the '67 set is in a high-number series and shows a prospective Hall of Famer, but it's only $250. And the prospective Hall of Famer, Rod Carew, was certainly no slouch. Only Ty Cobb won more batting titles. Carew hit .388 in 1977, the second-highest batting average in baseball since 1941. He could steal bases and rap out extra-base hits and someone said he could bunt every time up and still win a batting title. If Seaver was the dominant pitcher of his day Carew was the dominant hitter.

So if Carew's rookie card and Seaver's rookie card are in the same set and number series, why is one $750 and one $250?

Oh, New York, maybe.

It's a fact of baseball-card life that cards of players who play in New York are worth more than cards of players who don't play in New York. It's because there are so many more collectors in the New York metro area than anywhere else, but it gets a little strange having to justify why a rookie card of a Yankee pitcher who's destined to spend his entire career in middle relief in Columbus is worth more than the rookie card of a hot-shot power hitter for the Texas Rangers.

Tom Seaver was—and is—so popular in New York, both for his insurance-salesman/pro-golfer persona and his World Series heroics, that his card has been pushed up to big-time levels.

Rod Carew was barely popular in Minnesota, where he bought his ticket out by accusing Twins' owner Calvin Griffith of racism, and not much more popular in California, where he was expected to lead the Angels to the World Series but didn't.

There's no way to work out the New York factor in Seaver's card, or work some of that into Carew's card. That's just the way values in the card market are shaped. But as Cooperstown time nears for Carew, people are going to want a good Carew rookie card, and they're going to realize it's not that easy to find one. That's when you start chuckling.

Paul's Score: 24

Kit's Score: 30

TOTAL SCORE: 54

1971 Topps
Bert Blyleven

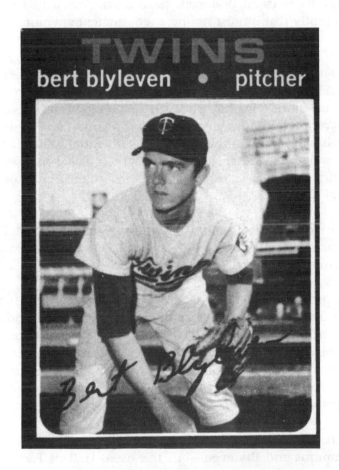

82

When baseball fans don't talk about pitchers who will someday be elected to the Hall of Fame, the first name they don't mention is Don Sutton. After not mentioning Sutton, they might not mention Jim Kaat or Tommy John. But after that, the name they're sure to not mention is Bert Blyleven.

Hey, don't look now, but Bert Blyleven is a very, very strong candidate for the Hall of Fame. He has every quality a Hall of Fame pitcher needs except outright dominance, and so many pitchers who weren't outright dominant have been elected to Cooperstown recently that it must not be a requirement anymore.

Blyleven is a certain Hall of Famer very much in the Sutton mold. Sutton won 324 games, and won 20 or more once. Blyleven has won 271 and counting, and won 20 or more once. Sutton has more wins but Blyleven will have more strikeouts. Both have pitched on pennant-winning teams. Though neither pitcher has ever truly pitched up to his potential, both have the numbers that demand enshrinement, which makes you wonder what they could have done if they had pitched up to their potential.

Blyleven's rookie card is in the 1971 Topps set. The 1971 Topps set is a massive thing, 752 cards, and about as easy to complete as the Great American Novel.

The big problem with the 1971 set is the borders. The '71s were the first big set to have black borders. As collectors found after playing around with their '71s, black borders don't stay uniformly black very long. Little pieces of the black border break off around the edges. Finding '71s with nice sharp borders that haven't been touched up with a Sharpie or trimmed down into '71 minis is tough.

Only a few significant rookies are in the '71 set—Steve Garvey, Ted Simmons and Blyleven—but the usual Hall of Famers are there in force, along with the best card of Ed Spezio you'll ever see and a high-number series that's just hard as heck to find.

Blyleven's card is in the first series, so it's no problem tracking one down. The problem is tracking one down in nicely centered, unchipped form. When you do, expect to pay about $20. That's up from $7 a couple of years ago, and in comparison to the Steve Garvey rookie ($75, up $20 from two years ago) that's more than reasonable.

Okay, so Bert Blyleven won't get in the Hall of Fame until they put in Don Sutton, and figure out what to do with Ferguson Jenkins and Jim Kaat and Rollie Fingers, and do something about Jim Bunning, and induct Steve Carlton. But Blyleven's still pitching. He's not through yet. His card's not through yet. Now's a real good time to buy it.

Paul's Score: 24

Kit's Score: 30

TOTAL SCORE: 54

1988 O-Pee-Chee
Delino DeShields

83

bout the only people who know about O-Pee-Chee cards are the people who collect O-Pee-Chee cards, and there aren't many of them because there aren't many O-Pee-Chee cards to collect. But if there were more O-Pee-Chee cards there probably wouldn't be more O-Pee-Chee collectors, because O-Pee-Chee cards are Canadian, and baseball is American, and there's something un-American about a Canadian baseball card.

O-Pee-Chee cards are Topps cards manufactured in Canada under license from Topps. The first O-Pee-Chee baseball cards were made in 1965. Sometimes the sets have as many cards as Topps sets, but usually an O-Pee-Chee set has fewer cards. Fewer cards in the set, more stars, and a higher percentage of stars to commons. You can say worse things about a set than it has a high percentage of stars to commons.

Until 1970, when bilingual backs were introduced, the cards were identical to Topps cards except for a small "Printed In Canada" line. O-Pee-Chee's front design has always been identical to Topps, except O-Pee-Chee is partial to a line reading "Traded To Whatever Team" instead of an airbrush job on cards of traded players. Back design has been identical (except for the bilingual stuff) every year except 1971, when high-number-series' backs were identical but low-number backs had a different design. Most of the special cards and some of the peripheral issues carry over from Topps to O-Pee-Chee. You'll find O-Pee-Chee deckle-edge cards and superstar posters and stickers and team checklists and box panels—all printed in fewer quantities than Topps cards, and all about as neglected as a mainline issue can get stateside.

While you can find plenty of players who are in Topps sets but not in O-Pee-Chee sets, there aren't many players who are in O-Pee-Chee sets but not in Topps sets. But in 1988 O-Pee-Chee did something insidious. It printed four cards of Montreal and Toronto's top 1987 draft picks and inserted them into its set. The cards show the players in the garb of their teams, and they're legitimate rookie cards in every way. The only thing they aren't is American.

The lineup of players is excellent, too, considering only four players are in the subset. There's the Expos' Nathan Minchey ("Now With Braves," as O-Pee-Chee might say), a top pitching prospect; the Blue Jays' Alex Sanchez, a better pitching prospect who made it to the majors briefly in 1989; the Jays' Derek Bell, their top outfield prospect in an organization full of top outfield prospects; and the Expos' Delino DeShields, the best pure shortstop prospect to come along in years, and one of the best prospects in baseball, period.

DeShields, who turned down a full-ride scholarship to Villanova to play baseball, was passed over in the rookie rush of '89 Bowman sets and Big cards and Upper Deck issues. But he has the potential to be a great ballplayer, and certainly a hot rookie. When that happens, people will come looking for his rookie card. Imagine their surprise when they discover it's in the '88 O-Pee-Chee set. DeShields may not turn the country on to O-Pee-Chee cards all by his lonesome, but he and Bell and Sanchez will raise public consciousness of the Canadian issues by a factor of five or six, and that will pump up the prices of these cards, which are still hanging in the 50 cents–75 cents range.

Best guesstimates are that 11 Topps cards are printed for every O-Pee-Chee card. The scarcity factor combined with the desirability factor make the '88 O-Pee-Chee set a true snoring sleeper. And Delino DeShields its best log-sawing card of all.

Paul's Score: 21

Kit's Score: 33

TOTAL SCORE: 54

1976 Topps
Andre Dawson

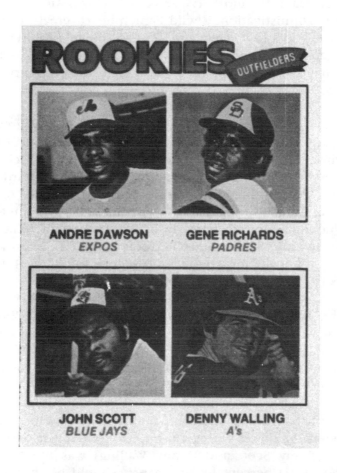

84

ow here's a card to play with just a little, even if it is priced about 10 percent higher than it ought to be. Andre Dawson had the great good fortune of playing the first 11 years of his career in Montreal. Montreal, Canada. That place where you bought postcards and everyone pretended that they didn't know English.

(You've probably read the same paragraph in scores of stories about Montreal ballplayers, only instead of the phrase "great good fortune" those stories have "misfortune." Look at it this way: Montreal is the most civilized city in North America. It has European sophistication, a wild French heart, great museums, great bars, and a low crime rate. It's easy to get around in, and it's gorgeous. There are worse places to play in the majors, and we'd name them, except they just happen to be pretty good places to buy books.)

While Andre Dawson played in Montreal and put up great big batting averages and nice pear-shaped home-run and RBI totals and ellipsoidal stolen-base numbers every year, and wrecked his knees on the Astroturf, nobody noticed. His baseball card went nowhere. People knew about the "Dream Outfield" of Ellis Valentine, Warren Cromartie and Dawson for a while, but after Valentine and Cromartie got their brains stuck in the retractable roof at Olympic Stadium people forgot about Dawson again. The only thing that broke the radio silence for Andre Dawson was his trade to the Chicago Cubs.

Ah, sure! The Cubs! Andre Dawson! Hits .375—no, .425—no, .650—at Wrigley! Bad knees! Day baseball! Andre Dawson! All of a sudden, everybody was an Andre Dawson fan. And overnight, and if not overnight then next-day air, Dawson's cards ballooned in price.

A nice little balloon, actually. Before the trade Dawson's rookie card (which he shares with good-hit, bad-field outfielders Gene Richards, Tony Scott and Denny Walling) was $6. Now it's $35—about 10 percent higher than it should be, but still in definite buyable range.

Here's why Dawson's rookie card is in a buyable range at $35 and Murphy's rookie card isn't in a buyable range at $60: Murphy's card costs $25 more than Dawson's. But Dawson has better career numbers. Murphy may have two MVP awards, but Dawson has one. And Dawson also has more hits, more runs batted in, more doubles, more triples, more stolen bases, a higher batting average, and more fielding awards. When it comes Hall of Fame time the sportswriters will forget all about the fact that Murphy played where millions could see him every night and Dawson couldn't.

Andre Dawson's card is every bit as ugly as Murphy's, but it's more buyable. And if you're going to buy ugly cards, you might as well buy the buyable ones.

Paul's Score: 23

Kit's Score: 30

TOTAL SCORE: 53

1988 Fleer
Jerry Browne
(Bob Brower)

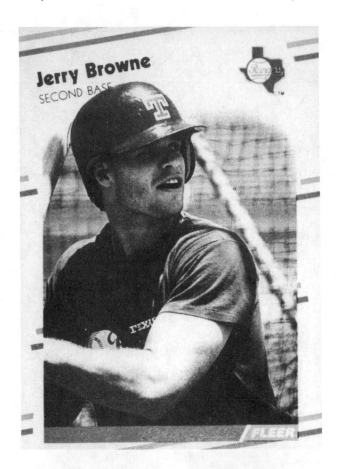

85

leer doesn't make the only errors on baseball cards, just the least intelligent errors. There's no excuse for a company whose business consists of making bubble gum and knowing what every player in baseball looks like to mistake Don Hood for Pete Vuckovich like they did in 1981. Mistaking Pete Vuckovich for a javelina, maybe. But not Don Hood. There's no excuse for Fleer mistaking Bill Travers for Jerry Augustine that same year. Granted, both Augustine and Travers look like extras from *Plan Nine From Outer Space*, but they don't look like each other. While part of it's the photographer's fault—photographers identify the players on the slides they send in—since when has a successful business been based on believing what photographers say? The ultimate responsibility for determining if that really is Kevin Romine or Randy Kutcher or a mountain gorilla rests with Fleer. And Fleer has been worse than any other cardmaker at properly exercising that responsibility.

Case in point: In the 1988 Fleer set the cards of two players show two other players, and not the players the cards are supposed to show. The card of Keith Moreland shows a ballplayer bunting who might be Keith Moreland. Actually, it's Jody Davis. But the photo doesn't look that much like either Moreland or Davis, and the idea of either of those ballplayers bunting is so far-fetched that Fleer might be forgiven the momentary confusion.

A better case in point: The 1988 Fleer Jerry Browne card does not show Jerry Browne. The editor of *Baseball Cards* magazine claims to have been the first person in the country to notice this error, though he makes no claims to any vast storehouses of baseball knowledge. He just knows the difference between a white man and a black man.

Jerry Browne is black. The player shown on Jerry Browne's 1988 Fleer card is not black. Considering Jerry Browne was one of Fleer's 1987 Major League Prospects, Fleer should have caught the error immediately. Fleer didn't. Its early-run cards have a picture of Bob Brower on Jerry Browne's cards.

Fleer corrected its error less than one-fifth of the way into its 1988 press run. The uncorrected Browne/Brower error cards are priced at $3.50. That's more than reasonable, and when you consider that Browne/Brower error cards were $1.50 six months ago, that's a price that won't stick around long. As an approximate final number of Browne/Brower error cards is determined—and it's going to be small—the price will move up. This ought to be a $10 card within 18 months.

Its companion, the Moreland/Davis error, is just as good a buy. It just isn't as stupid.

The story doesn't end there. Believe it or not, that wasn't the last time Fleer made that same mistake that year. Its 1988 Update set includes a card of the Pirates' Tommy Gregg that actually shows the Pirates' Randy Milligan. Gregg is white. Milligan is—you guessed it—black. Old habits die hard.

Paul's Score: 24

Kit's Score: 29

TOTAL SCORE: 53

1965 Topps
Jim Hunter

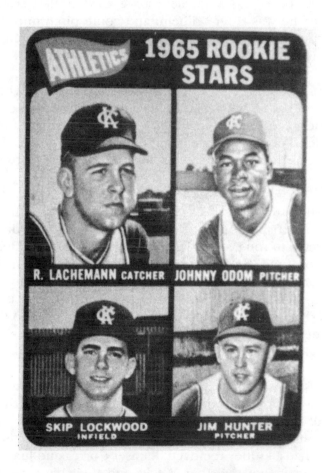

86

I

f you liked the story about the 1963 Topps rookies, you'll love the story of the 1965 Topps rookies. It's like *Ghostbusters*, with chewing tobacco.

Just like the '63s, there's the valuable rookie card, and then there's the rookie card you should buy, even if it is as ugly as 25-year-old bubble gum.

The valuable rookie card shows Fritz Ackley and Steve Carlton. It used to be a real valuable rookie card until Carlton got convinced he was Hoyt Wilhelm and could pitch until he was 70, no matter what his slider kept telling him. Mostly his slider kept telling him, "So long. See you later. Downtown."

The valuable rookie card is worth about $200, and might go up an extra $50 or so when Carlton is elected to the Hall of Fame, but in the meantime it'll just keep cruising along with the 1965 set, which generally looks great but isn't anywhere near as expensive as the '66 and '67 sets, for a couple of reasons named Tom Seaver and high numbers.

The rookie card that isn't as valuable belongs to Catfish Hunter. Now, the Catfish is one of those pitchers who wouldn't have been elected to the Hall of Fame if they just elected numbers to the Hall of Fame. He won a couple hundred games but not too many more than that, and didn't strike out as many guys as Jim Bunning. But he was the money pitcher of the last great baseball dynasty, the Oakland A's of the mid-1970s, and that got him some extra credit in the sportswriters' book. Besides, he did a heck of a light-beer commercial.

The Catfish was a bonus baby, a big bonus baby who after he got his check promptly went out and shot himself in the foot. Bonus babies were (and are) always good for some kind of behavior like that. Rick Reichardt of the Angels got his bonus and then had a kidney removed. Ramser Correa and Juan Nieves of the Brewers got their big checks and their big cars and the *haciendas* for their mothers, and then tossed some roofing tacks in their rotator cuffs. None of these players were the same players after their injuries as they had been before, which makes you wonder if they ever were the players they were before their injuries. But only the Catfish got better.

Catfish Hunter's rookie card is in the 1965 Topps set, and it really is remarkably ugly. There are four players on the card—

Hunter's Swingin' A's buddy Blue Moon Odom, Skip Lockwood and someday manager Rene Lachemann—and every one of them looks like something you might do at home with your paint-by-number kit after a tumblerful of Famous Grouse.

Even so, a couple of facts remain despite our efforts. The card does show a Hall of Famer under all that paint. Steve Carlton is going to be a Hall of Famer, but he isn't one yet. The Hunter card is $110 cheaper than the Carlton card, and only $40 more than the Tony Perez rookie. Perez isn't going to make the Hall of Fame unless the Hall of Fame decides to induct about 40 players at once. The Hunter card is in a semi-tough high-number series, and it's a challenge to find one with good centering and a little bit of gloss and without a couple of tons of pack wax smeared across the face. You can never go wrong with high-number cards of Hall of Famers. All the numbers are in your favor. Even if the Catfish's numbers weren't all that hot.

Paul's Score: 23

Kit's Score: 30

TOTAL SCORE: 53

1963 Topps
Willie Stargell

We now join *Classroom Of The Air* already in progress.

Problem: Two great rookie cards are in the 1963 Topps set, and neither of them is Pete Rose. One great rookie card is in the '63 Topps set, and that is Pete Rose. Which statement is true?

Solution: According to the laws of logic, the negation of A and not B is equal to not A and B, plus the square root of two and a player to be named later. Both statements are true.

The Pete Rose is the great rookie card in the '63 set because it's the rookie card of Pete Rose. The Tony Oliva rookie card is one of the two great rookie cards in the '63 set mainly because it's so cheap, and the Willie Stargell rookie card is the other great rookie card in the '63 set mainly because Stargell was so good.

Stargell was good, and modern fans get so wrapped up in Stargell's teddy-bear persona and his "We Are Family" leadership style—the power of positive thinking, with a backbeat—and his TV commercials and his gig with the Pittsburgh Symphony and the whole Stargell-as-institution schtick that they forget just how good, how consistently excellent, Stargell was throughout his playing career.

Stargell was no one-dimensional player, along the lines of Killebrew or Kiner. He hit .282 for his career, lashed out 2,232 hits and 475 home runs, and drove in 1,540 runs. He had the handicap of hitting in Forbes Field, hardly the favorite ballpark of any left-handed hitter, yet he knocked seven balls over the roof at Forbes. Only nine other players have done it *once*. Stargell was in double figures in home runs every year from 1963 to 1980; he hit 20 or more homers every year from 1964–1979, except for 1977, when injuries limited him to 63 games.

There. That was Willie Stargell the player. Now maybe you can start thinking about him in the same mental breath as Roberto Clemente or Willie McCovey.

But there was always more to Willie Stargell than numbers. There was always that leadership, that persona, that charisma. Pete Rose has a persona and displays some of the qualities of leadership, but charisma has always been as foreign to him as a permanent wave. And charisma keeps the values of cards strong in the long run.

A Stargell rookie's not cheap—$200—but even at that price you can buy four to one Rose rookie. You might not want to buy four, but one wouldn't be a bad idea. It's a homely card—it looks like something a mad scientist cooked up with four shrunken heads and an old piece of pool-table felt—but it's done a tremendous job of appreciating in the last two-plus years. It's moved from $48 to $200, and $200 may not be an upper bound. It's in a relatively common number series, and it's surrounded by high-priced cards (Clemente, Rose and Duke Snider are all within 25 cards) and a few bargains (the Dave McNally rookie at a cheap $9, and the Rusty Staub rookie at a not-bad $25), so people know where it is. And as memories of the 1979 World Series and Stargell's heroics begin to take on mythical proportions more and more collectors will come around to this card. It's a good card to come around to—especially right now.

Paul's Score: 23

Kit's Score: 30

TOTAL SCORE: 53

W551
Cobb and Ruth

88

I t's time to indict strip cards again. Where shall we start?

How about here: they're small. Strip cards are often smaller than tobacco cards, and tobacco cards are small. Or here: quality. Most strip cards are just strips of paper with a picture on one side and nothing but paper on the other. The pictures are described in most price guides as "crude drawings," which does a disservice to the other crude drawings of the world. Statistical information beyond the player's name and his team does not exist. Small wonder collectors don't really bark for strip cards.

Against that gloomy backdrop, what good is there to say about strip cards? How about: they're cheap. Sure, it's like saying grasshoppers make an inexpensive dinner meat that's quick to fix and oh-so-good for you, but grasshoppers are an acquired taste, just like strip cards. If the world gives you grasshoppers, you make lemonade. If the world gives you strip cards, you make lemonade. You learn to appreciate the bright drawings and hand-colored pictures as quaint, as American Primitive art from the same school as Grandma Moses, albeit from kindergarten. And you learn that you don't have to shell out $1,000 for a Ruth card or $800 for a Cobb card, and you can even get a card of the two of them together.

Strip cards do capture some of the tougher players of the day in their delightful color-by-number style. The 1919 W514 strip-card set has cards of seven of the eight Chicago Black Sox, including the only strip card of Shoeless Joe Jackson. And get this: The Jackson card is cheaper than a new car! Only $80. Wonderful things, these strip cards, huh?

It gets better. How about a strip that gives you Ty Cobb and Babe Ruth right next to one another? You bet. They're right there in tandem in the 1922 W551 set.

Admittedly, the Ruth likeness is barely close to Ruth, and other than the grip on his bat, Cobb looks nothing like Cobb. And with Ruth and Cobb representing a full one-fifth of the set (which also contains Hall of Famers Dave Bancroft, Frank Baker, Casey Stengel, Tris Speaker, George Sisler, Jess Barnes and Walter Johnson), the W551 set is otherwise unimportant. But, hey, here's a set that consists of 90 percent Hall of Famers that catalogs for $600, less than the cost of any one of these Hall of Famers elsewhere. And here's a pair of cards, Cobb and Ruth, that are found as a pair and that you can have for approximately $500. A deal? A deal. A fascinating item no matter the price and a swell item at this price.

Paul's Score: 33

Kit's Score: 19

TOTAL SCORE: 52

1973 Topps
Bob Boone

A s long as you're taking your spouse to the dead-and-down livestock man to buy **Pudge Fisk** rookie cards, might as well take your pets and all your distant relatives that you never hear from anyway except for weddings and funerals and those darn Christmas letters ("Well, another wonderful year has whizzed past us so fast," they always start, which is undoubtedly true, because they don't have to read their own Christmas letter) and get a little extra cash. You'll need it to spend on a couple of semi-sure things from the 1973 set.

The real sure thing in the 1973 set is the Mike Schmidt rookie, but real sure things are usually no fun because they cost too much—$300 in Schmidt's case. Way too much. The semi-sure things are much more fun because you could lose. Isn't that fun? Doesn't the idea of losing a good chunk of change appeal to you? No? Then spend your money on semi-sure things that don't cost so much. Then you'll only be out an eight-ounce wedge of change if you lose.

How about $25? Can you afford to spend $25 on a semi-sure thing? You can? Good for you. His name's Bob Boone.

Sure. Booney. The catcher pitchers most like to have catch them. The all-time games-caught leader. The great defensive catcher and okay hitter (.253 lifetime). The son of Ray Boone, the three-time Gold Glove winner and two-time assist leader, and the guy behind the plate for six division winners. If Brooks Robinson can get into the Hall of Fame primarily on his glove and Rabbit Maranville can get into the Hall of Fame on his glove and Ray Schalk can get into the Hall on his head and his glove, certainly Bob Boone can get into the Hall of Fame somehow. Sounds like a sure thing to us.

The only thing that makes Bob Boone a semi-sure thing and not a sure thing is actually a couple of things. One of them is named Carlton Fisk and the other is named Walker Cooper. Walker Cooper, the great catcher for the Cardinals and Giants in the 1940s, really deserves a shot at the Hall of Fame. (For that matter, so does Sherm Lollar, the only catcher of the 1950s to nudge Yogi Berra off of an all-star team.) Before Cooperstown can deal with Bob Boone it has to deal with Fisk, Lollar and Cooper. (The Veterans' Committee gets to deal with Lollar and Cooper.)

Hey, what do you expect for $7.25? If you buy Bob Boone's rookie card expecting to make money on it, you have to believe the baseball writers will give more weight to the fact that Boone caught more games than any other catcher in history than they will to the fact that he was not Lou Gehrig. If you buy Bob Boone's card just to have it, you'll get a high-series card that's more attractive than most multi-player rookie cards and can also fill you in on what Skip Jutze and Mike Ivie were up to in 1973.

Either way, it's not too much money out of your pocket. And it is a semi-sure thing. Semi-sure, mind you.

Paul's Score: 20

Kit's Score: 32

TOTAL SCORE: 52

1982 Fleer
John Littlefield
Error

John Littlefield
PADRES • PITCHER

leer didn't make more errors in its 1982 set than it did in its '81 set. That wouldn't be possible. To make more errors than the '81 set would have required making an entire error set. And that would have sounded too much like a discount-stereo-store ad for our taste. "Oops! Sorry! We goofed! We undersold! We overbought! We didn't read *The Baseball Encyclopedia*! We thought that Billy Travers was Jerry Augustine! We thought Pete Vuckovich was Don Hood! We thought that Al Hrabosky stands only five feet one! Now we're going to pass those errors on to you!" Nah. It was bad enough seeing Stan Papi listed as a pitcher.

While Fleer didn't make more errors in its '82 set than its '81 set, it made bigger errors. It called Al Hrabosky "All" and listed his height as 5'1" instead of 5'10". It took three tries to get that card right, with the "All" Hrabosky/5'1" version cataloging at $20. But Fleer's biggest error was taking journeyman right-hander John Littlefield, turning around his picture, and making him a left-hander.

Mistakes like this happen all the time in baseball cards, and aren't inherently valuable. When Topps flipped the negative on Hank Aaron's card in 1957 or Jim Gantner's card in 1987, that didn't make those cards automatically three or four times more valuable than any other Aaron or Gantner cards. The only thing that can make those cards more valuable than they would be normally is *if the card company subsequently issues a corrected variety.*

In John Littlefield's case Fleer did, quickly. The error was caught early in the press run, the presses were stopped and the cards corrected. But cases and packs with the error card were shipped.

This is the classic scenario that makes a classic error, and this is Fleer's classic error. The card has a $150 catalog value but could easily sell for three or four times that. It almost never comes on the market, and it sells for more than catalog value whenever it does. The Littlefield error ranks with the Donruss Opening Day Barry Bonds/Johnny Ray error as one of the most significant errors of the '80s.

Card companies hate errors, and they hate the way collectors collect errors. But collectors aren't collecting errors; collectors are collecting scarcity. Collectors want to have something no one else does, but they want to be able to get it when they want to get it, and get rid of it when they want to get rid of it. The Littlefield card is the perfect card for them. The only hard part is finding one.

Paul's Score: 23

Kit's Score: 28

TOTAL SCORE: 51

1981 Donruss
Tim Raines

91

Looking back at what there is to look back on, Donruss looks like it got off easy in 1981. While Fleer did all the dirty lawsuit work and paid off all the lawyers and sweated out the circuit courts, all Donruss had to do was be around at the end with its baseball cards. Topps never named Donruss in a lawsuit, or vice versa; Donruss was just there, trailing in Fleer's wake.

Reality wasn't like that. Fleer was the leader because Fleer had initiated the first action in 1974 and yes, Fleer was bigger. Topps knew that any court decision that applied to Fleer would have to apply to Donruss. If Topps sued Fleer and won, it could apply that legal precedent to prevent Donruss from issuing baseball cards. And beating Fleer for the sake of beating Fleer was important to Topps.

While Donruss wanted to make baseball cards, and had applied to the Major League Baseball Players Association for permission to do a card set, it was just as surprised as Fleer by how quickly the MLBPA came out of the chute once it decided it wanted competition in the baseball-card business. Donruss was not at all ready to do baseball cards when the time came to do baseball cards. The 1981 Donruss set is as much a big nutty nut of a set as the 1981 Fleer set, with the same snapshot photographic philosophy and the same batch of wild streaks.

The 1981 Fleer and Donruss sets are a lot alike in a lot of ways: photography, design, quality. When you look at these two sets you wonder what Topps was so worried about, and you marvel at the strides these two companies have made since then. The 1981 Donruss set is a horrible thing by present-day standards. It was probably a horrible thing by 1981 standards, too, but the hobby was more desperate for competition back then. If the 1981 Donruss set would have been issued, looking like it does, in 1989, it'd be laughed right off the market, or at the very least, packaged in boxes of Slimee Crunchees cereal or cans of 10W-40 or something.

Donruss had to get photographs for its '81 set in a hurry, so it went to Mike Aronstein. In 1976 Aronstein had taken the photos for a set of his own devising commonly called the SSPC set. Later on he formed TCMA and revolutionized the minor-league card market. But neither SSPC or TCMA were renowned for their breathtaking photos. Aronstein and his photographers shot mostly in Comiskey Park and Wrigley Field, in near darkness and heavy overcast, but did a pretty good job considering. The photography doesn't get any help from the paper, which is lousy, even by Donruss' thin-is-in standards. The print job is awful. Backs contain just a handful of statistics and a few career highlights. Names are spelled wrong; players and teams are mixed up. Like the 1981 Fleer set, the 1981 Donruss set must have made collectors ask: "Doesn't anyone here know *anything* about baseball?"

The answer, not surprisingly, was yes and no. The people who produced the 1981 Donruss set knew a little about baseball but not that much, and didn't know much at all about photo quality, paper or printing, or lawsuits, or temporary restraining orders, or licensing arrangements, or royalties. The most knowledgeable people knew about the SSPC set, which was supposed to be the first of many but turned out to be a one-off when Topps made some low belches in its direction. The Donruss people would get better, but not right away. They had to learn what they did wrong before they could do anything right. And Donruss did a lot of things wrong in 1981.

Donruss got its set out; give the company credit for that. But the interesting thing is that they didn't get it out that much. The 1981 Donruss set is not common. It's priced level with the Fleer set at $25—on principle, probably—but it's scarcer. The people who put it out have said recently the '81 Donruss set ought to be worth more because they know how few of them were made. Since the people who made the first Donruss set are no longer with Donruss, they don't have much to gain by saying the set is scarce. Assuming they're telling the truth, there's no reason why the '81 Donruss set should be $35 and the much more common Topps set should be $90.

The whole set's a recommended buy, but one of the best single cards in the '81 Donruss set is the Tim Raines card. It's not listed as his rookie card, but it is; the official Tim Raines rookie card is in the 1981 Topps set, but there's no reason for the '81 Topps Raines to be a rookie card and the '81 Donruss Raines not to be a rookie card. The Donruss Raines is a more attractive card, though not by much. If the '81 Topps Raines didn't show Bobby Pate and Roberto Ramos in addition to Raines, it'd get the nod, but as a rule a card that shows little photos of three players cannot beat a card that shows a big photo of one player, no matter what that one big photo looks like. The Donruss Raines is at $5 and rising, though not very fast. Raines' cards are generally undervalued, and this one's a little more undervalued than most. Canada again. This card has the potential to triple in value in three years.

The 1981 Donruss set deserves a little more respect, not for being a great set or for being the first set from a company that would eventually turn out some great sets, but for not turning many of its type out on the world right away. That would come later.

Paul's Score: 23

Kit's Score: 27

TOTAL SCORE: 50

1983 Donruss
Ryne Sandberg

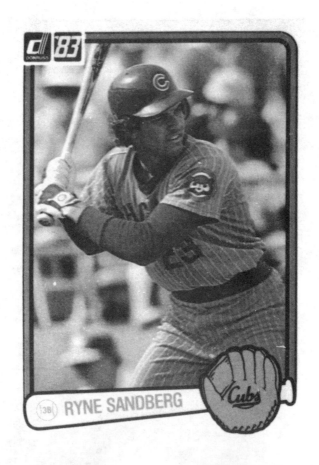

92

There are three significant cards of three significant players in the three semi-significant 1983 sets. Sandberg comes in third, but not by as much as the numbers might indicate.

By 1983 Donruss had its baseball-card lines all learned. Donruss came out with its first Diamond Kings that year, and what Diamond Kings they were: Hall of Famers Willie Stargell, Carl Yastrzemski and Johnny Bench, and future Hall of Famers Rollie Fingers, Steve Carlton, Reggie Jackson, Jim Palmer, and Joe Morgan. (Looking for a bargain? The most expensive of these Diamond Kings costs 80 cents. They're just scaled-down reproductions of just-okay paintings by baseball artist Dick Perez, but Perez has a reputation as a sports artist—that fine sub-genre that brought us such beauts as Leroy Nieman—that's inflating a foot an hour, and his Perez-Steele postcards and Celebration cards are genuine collectibles. These Diamond Kings could be the perfect combination of undervalued cards, overvalued artist and Hall of Fame players. Or they just could be 80-cent cud commons.)

Donruss also put the last refinements on its backs in 1983, and hand it to Donruss: come Score and Upper Deck and high water and all sorts of changes in the baseball-card industry, Donruss has kept its backs virtually unchanged for the last six years. Call it good old rock-ribbed American traditionalism, but the real reason Donruss hasn't changed its backs in six years, a Donrussian told us, is because no one looks at card backs anyway. Silly us. We thought people looked at card backs. But Donruss has survey data to prove its side and we don't, so we must be wrong.

Donruss, like Fleer and Topps, has three key cards in its 1983 set: Ryne Sandberg, Tony Gwynn and Wade Boggs. As we mentioned, Sandberg is the least of the three, but is probably the best value. Sandberg is an exceptionally popular player, with matinee-idol looks and national-TV marquee value. He's a solid hitter, a perennial all-star and arguably the best second baseman in the game. He may not have the batting titles Gwynn and Boggs have, but he has a Most Valuable Player award neither one of them have. And the going rate of exchange at Cooperstown is three batting titles equal one MVP award.

When you figure Sandberg gives you all that for $7 in the '83 Donruss set, and when you figure what $7 doesn't give you in later Donruss sets, and when you further figure that that price

279

hasn't budged in two years though Sandberg certainly has, the Sandberg rookie seems like a real buy. And when you further figure how many Sandberg rookies you could have bought with the money you spent on that moosehide meatloaf and Spam cheesecake you had for lunch, you're probably going to be sick.

Paul's Score: 21

Kit's Score: 28

TOTAL SCORE: 49

W517 Ted Lyons

93

kay, let's face it: Strip cards aren't for everybody. They aren't even for all the people who know what strip cards are and can name the different types, and there aren't many people like that. The busy collector might just thumb through that section of the catalog at a glance, figuring, "Oh, they're ugly," or, "Oh, they're small," or, "Oh, they're flimsy," or, "Oh, their color scheme clashes with my suit." That collector would be making a mistake. Strip cards *do* go with that suit. It's just a matter of wearing the proper tie.

On the other hand, strip cards are often ugly and small and flimsy. They were made to be small and flimsy at least when they were printed more than 60 years ago. Strip cards were usually printed on long strips or rolls, like tickets for carnival rides. Storekeepers would give them away with purchases or package them with certain products. We still have an awful lot to learn about the different kinds of strip cards, where they came from and what they were used for and even how many players are in some of the strip-card sets.

But strip cards have some awfully good potential, if you want old cards that are still relatively inexpensive. The very things collectors have seen as drawbacks to strip cards—being small and flimsy and ugly—can be advantages. And they're really not that ugly.

They're really not all that small, either. The W517 is a healthy sized set by early-card standards; in fact, their three-inch-by-four-inch size is actually bigger than most "regular" cards of the day. While we know the size of and think we know all the players from the W517 set, we know just a very little bit more about the cards. We know by their perforations that they came in a large sheet and were divided into individual cards. We know the paper quality is actually quite good, and much better than most strip-card issues. We know that the W517s are unusual because they have pictures instead of rudimentary drawings, and that the pictures come in sepiatone (less desirable) and other colors (more desirable).

The W517 set is heavy in big-name stars from 1931, and it's scarce. But that scarcity hasn't translated into high prices. The set has two Babe Ruths and a Gehrig, and they're pricey, but second-echelon Hall of Famers like Ted Lyons are only about $75 each, when you can find them.

The W517 set gives you the chance to buy a period Ruth or Gehrig without having to resort to a truly rough strip card or spend more on a card than you spent on your car, or buy a Ted Lyons card for pin money. The set still has an air of mystery about it. Its quality makes it at least the equal of most non-strip sets. The cards' combination of affordability and scarcity may not be around long.

Paul's Score:　26

Kit's Score:　23

TOTAL SCORE:　49

1988 Score Glossy
Gregg Jefferies

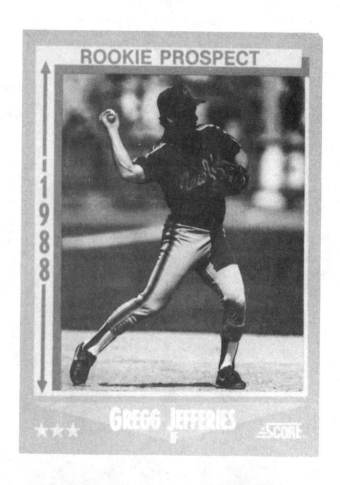

94

nce upon a time there was a baseball-card collector and a raven. The baseball-card collector said, "I like to buy rookie cards and make money off of them." The raven said, "I like to perch on dead animals and pluck their eyeballs out and eat them, and eat their liver and heart." The baseball-card collector said, "We're really not that far apart then." And the raven agreed.

The baseball-card collector: "I think I will buy 1988 Donruss Gregg Jefferies cards, because Gregg Jefferies is a great rookie, and a New York Met rookie besides, and that means his card will go up in value."

"Nevermore!" said the raven, a little too predictably. "Jefferies' Donruss rookie card is already $6.50. That's better than three cents for every point of his batting average. How much higher do you think his card can go, brother baseball-card collector?"

"But what am I supposed to do?" said the baseball-card collector. "I can't perch on dead animals and pluck their eyeballs out. I have to buy rookie cards and make money off of them. And I like Gregg Jefferies. He's a great rookie, and a New York Met besides."

"My gosh!" the raven said, shaking his beak from side to side and rolling his black eyes up into his tiny black head. "Do I have to tell you everything? I can't believe you picked out the Kevin Scitzer rookie all by yourself. Don't you realize there's more than one Gregg Jefferies rookie?"

"Sure," said the collector, looking a little sheepish (which is the wrong thing to do around a raven). "There's the Fleer Gregg Jefferies, but—"

"And," said the raven, bobbing up and down. "And what else?"

"The Score Gregg Jefferies, but—"

"And," said the raven again. "And what else?"

"Sportflics?" the collector said, looking very sheepish and confused now. "Update sets? '89 Topps? I don't understand."

"Here, I'll give you a clue," the raven said, spreading his great wings. "Look at my feathers. What are they like? What do they have to do with baseball cards?"

The collector scratched his head. "Black? There's a black set?"

The raven squawked and cawed mightily.

"No, no, no, no!" he screamed. "*Glossy*, you fool! Glossy!"

"Oh, yeah," the collector said. "Glossy."

Things were silent a minute.

"You mean Fleer glossy?"

The raven just shook his head.

"You mean Score made a glossy set?"

The raven, detecting the smell of fresh three-day-old dead skunk, gave his feathers one last big shake and flew off to dinner, calling out, "CAW-ley! Buy Joe CAW-ley cards!" as he flew. The collector, who didn't realize that Score indeed made a glossy set in 1988, and that fewer than 3,000 were made, and that a Gregg Jefferies card from that set would be a marvelous buy, was pondering all this when he wandered out into traffic, was struck by a septic-tank pump truck, and died. The raven had left too soon.

MORAL: The smart bird knows the score. And the Score Glossy.

Paul's Score: 18

Kit's Score: 31

TOTAL SCORE: 49

1985 Donruss
Tom Seaver Error

95

ome people who do nothing but watch the baseball-card market for a living will tell you that as far as the recent stuff goes, the even-numbered years are the ones to go after. Buy all the 1984, 1986 and 1988 cards you can. Forget about 1985, 1987 and 1989. Nothing interesting ever came out of those years.

Well, that's just plain wrong. If your definition of something interesting is something that cost a dime when it was issued and $90 now, yes, you're right; there is nothing in the odd-numbered-year sets that's that kind of interesting. But if your definition of something interesting is something that's not worth now what it was when it was issued, and isn't worth a fraction of what it will be worth in a couple of years—maybe even a year—then the odd-numbered-year sets are every bit as interesting as the even-numbered-year ones. Maybe a little more interesting.

Take a look at just one odd-numbered-year set: the 1985 Donruss set. People would rather pay $225 for a 1984 Donruss set than $130 for a 1985 Donruss set because they think it's more interesting. But what does the '84 Donruss set have besides Don Mattingly? The first Donruss card of Darryl Strawberry? Heck, the 1985 Donruss set has the first Donruss cards of Dwight Gooden *and* Roger Clemens *and* Kirby Puckett, all reasonably priced, *and* the Orel Hershiser rookie, *and* one of the most interesting errors of the 1980s. Two errors, actually.

Word spread quickly in 1985 that something was wrong with the Tom Seaver card in the 1985 Donruss set. The pitcher wasn't Tom Seaver, and it was easy to tell that it wasn't Tom Seaver, because this pitcher was throwing left-handed. Tom Terrific was that, but left-handed he was not. The left-hander was Floyd Bannister, at that time one of the White Sox's top two starters.

While word spread quickly among collectors and dealers that Tom Seaver wasn't quite himself, it took its time getting back to Donruss. Donruss kept its presses cranking out Tom Seaver cards of Floyd Bannister well into the summer—a lifetime, by baseball-card production schedules. When the first corrected Seaver cards turned up—showing the proper Seaver, pitching right-handed—Donruss cards vaporized. One store in a city might have had them until word got around, then none at all would have them.

Setting values for corrected and uncorrected versions of an error card is tricky, because the numbers can break one of three ways: either the error is common and the corrected version is scarce, the corrected version is common and the error is scarce, or the two are about equally common or scarce. The *corrected* Seaver is scarce, but even today no one knows quite how scarce. Its catalog value is six times that of the uncorrected Seaver, but considering how late in the run the card was corrected, the price for the corrected version seems low. And with interest in error cards growing all the time, and Seaver's enshrinement in Cooperstown looming, it seems doubly low.

The Tom Seaver error is a fun card, and it has some value, too. Cards like this come around too seldom in the modern run of things.

Paul's Score: 14

Kit's Score: 35

TOTAL SCORE: 49

1977 Topps
Dale Murphy

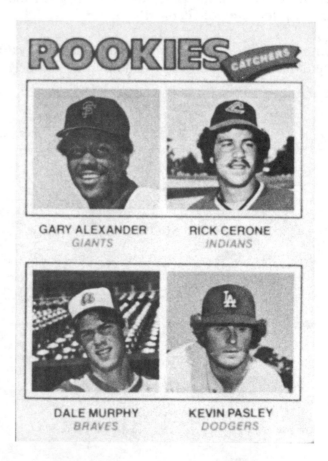

Afterter doing less than nothing with not much more than that in 1976 (how dull is the 1976 set? The most exciting card shows Steve Grilli, Craig Mitchell, Jose Sosa and George Throop), Topps walked up to the edge of a Grand Canyon of a new baseball era in 1977 and said, "Uh, I prefer K mart." Good old Topps.

Actually, the first replacements in the changing of the baseball-card guard arrived in 1977 on three big rookie cards whose distinctive price movements in the last couple of years say a lot about how the card market works, what goes up and why.

Two years ago the Rookie Catchers card that features Gary Alexander, Kevin Pasley, Rick Cerone and Dale Murphy was selling for $52, because Dale Murphy was *it*: center fielder and home-run hitter for America's Team 1982, the Atlanta Braves. Murph was coming off of an MVP year, or off of an off of an MVP year, or two, and he was white (still is), and he was one of the game's best good guys (still is), so his card should have been selling for almost twice the price of the Mattingly rookie. At that point it was a logical price.

But Dale Murphy has found a couple of obstacles on his superhighway from Rookie Catchers to Cooperstown. The first has been the ineptness of his team, the Atlanta Braves, and then their inability to find anyone who can hit to hit behind Murphy. The result has been fewer good pitches to hit, more walks, fewer hits, and more outs registered on bad pitches. Bob Horner may have looked and acted like the guy at the Snort 'N' Spit Bar who does both, simultaneously, while doing shake of the day and sinking the 11 ball in the corner pocket, but he was a frightening hitter to have hitting behind Dale Murphy. Once Horner left, Murphy was left to disprove the axiom: A man *can* be an island, if he hits cleanup for the Braves.

None of this leaves Murphy's rookie card anyplace good. Unless Murphy is traded—a very real—make that a *very*, very real—possibility—or unless the Braves develop a bona fide hit-behind-Murphy hitter, his card is at a high, and is more likely to move down from that high than achieve a new high. It's not one of the most attractive cards of all time, either, so unless you're an ugly-card collector or consider buying Dale Murphy cards a religious expense that you can take off your taxes, you'd best leave this one alone.

Paul's Score: 21

Kit's Score: 28

TOTAL SCORE: 49

1981 Fleer
Graig (Craig) Nettles

GRAIG NETTLES
THIRD BASE

9 7

I t took 26 years and a few hundred thousand dollars in legal fees, and a slew of threats and counterthreats and a couple of martyr sets, and a court judgment and a reversal and another judgment, but Topps' exclusive hold on baseball cards was broken in time for the 1981 season. The walls came tumbling down, sort of, and even though this is a book on individual baseball cards and not the baseball-card business in general, understanding why those walls came down might help you understand how the card market got to where it is today.

Fleer was no stranger to the trading-card business, though its desire to enter the baseball end of things seemed to run in streaks of three or four years. It made a Ted Williams set and all-time-greats sets and one truncated baseball set in the 1960s, and made some football cards, but then it low-keyed baseball cards until the early 1970s, when it came back bigger in the baseball-card business and issued two sets of World Series cards.

The World Series sets went over well, and so by 1974 Fleer was fully ready for an assault on Topps' baseball-card market. Fleer wanted to come out with sets of 5 × 7 patches, cards and photos. But it couldn't. It wasn't allowed to. And for a change, Topps wasn't even the real culprit.

The real culprit was the Major League Baseball Players' Association. It didn't exist the last time Fleer tried to enter the baseball-card market, but it had had an agreement with Topps since 1968, which gave Topps the exclusive right to market cards just about any darn way it wanted to. Fleer was shut out of the market, so Fleer sued.

The U.S. District Court held for Fleer. The Third Circuit Court of Appeals reversed. As far as the courts were concerned, Topps didn't have a monopoly, Fleer was still shut out, and they'd be shut out as long as Topps had its individual player contracts and its working agreement with the players' association.

If the courts shut out Fleer, and the agreements shut out Fleer, how'd Fleer ever get into the baseball-card business? One hint: It wasn't through the courts. By 1980, the players' association had convinced its members what it always believed: competition is good, because competition means more money for everybody. The MLBPA convinced its members to give it their individual rights, which Topps had traditionally taken pains to secure. The MLBPA then granted rights to make and sell cards to

Fleer and Donruss. There was only one caveat to the two licenses: Neither Donruss nor Fleer could sell its cards with candy, gum or any confectionary product. That was where Topps' exclusivity lay; those rights remained with Topps, and have to this day. Topps would later sue first the MLPBA and then Fleer, contending that Fleer and the MLBPA unfairly evaded Topps' exclusive agreements, but the courts would not go along with Topps this time. Through sheer Fleer persistence, the monopoly days ended for Topps in 1981.

It's really a shame that after all that travail Fleer's 1981 set is such a mess. Perhaps because Fleer slapped the set together in a hurry after getting its license, it's full of bad photographs. Errors run around like cockroaches in a tenement. Names are misspelled, photos are reversed, photos are switched, positions are goofed up, and weird little fingers show up on the backs of a handful of cards from the set. There are two Bill Travers cards and two Don Hood cards in the set because Fleer mistook Travers and Hood for other players (Jerry Augustine and Pete Vuckovich, respectively, neither of whom look anything like Bill Travers and Don Hood, respectively), and then thought it was easier to keep the photo and trash the rest of the card than vice versa.

Since Fleer had no shame and printed oodles of these cards and got them out everywhere, nothing in the set is worth much money. The set catalogs at $35, which isn't bad, considering it spent most of the decade at $15–$20. The most valuable error card in the set—the most valuable card in the set, period— shows Graig Nettles but reads "Craig" Nettles on the back. It's a fairly scarce card of a pretty good ballplayer, and it sells for $12. It's no hot hot hot young rookie or anything, but it's a great card if you're a Young Communist and into symbols of the class struggle, and a pretty good card otherwise. It should be a $25 card within two years, which ought to make the running bourgeoisie dog in all of us wag its little tail with joy. We know ours does.

Paul's Score: 21

Kit's Score: 28

TOTAL SCORE: 49

1962 Topps Babe Ruth/Hal Reniff/Hal Reniff

98

Here's the baseball-card equivalent of the seven-cent nickel. In case you don't remember the seven-cent nickel, it's in a Marx Brothers movie, *Animal Crackers*. You can buy a two-cent newspaper with the seven-cent nickel (at least you could back then) and get five cents back. One nickel, carefully used, could last a family a lifetime. And that's sort of the way it is with #139 in the 1962 Topps set.

Number 139 in the 1962 Topps set falls smack in the middle of a Babe Ruth subset. On one side are cards like "Babe Joins Yanks" and "The Famous Slugger," and on the other side are cards like "Gehrig And Ruth" and "The Twilight Years." It's the sort of trivialize-the-great subset that Topps specializes in and would later insist on doing for Hank Aaron and Pete Rose. Card #139 in this case was titled "Babe Hits 60," and you can just imagine what the card looked like.

Well, maybe you can't. Some of the time card #139 looked like you imagine, Babe Ruth looking up from his swing and everything, and some of the time it looked just like Hal Reniff, right down to having a picture of Reniff pitching on the front and the legend, "Hal Reniff-Pitcher-Yankees" down in the corner.

This was most unusual, even for Topps, which through the 1960s specialized in the inexplicable mistake. Why, for instance, would they show some other player as Tigers farmhand George Korince, and Tigers farmhand George Korince as some other player, all in the course of a couple of rookie cards? Why would they write on the back of Phillies rookie Dave Bennett's card, "This 18-year-old right-handed curve-baller is only 19 years old"? Why would they put a photo of the long-dead Ken Hubbs in the 1966 Topps set and call him Dick Ellsworth? Topps was real good in the 1960s. But they were never better than they were with Hal Reniff.

And it gets better. Once Topps realized it had issued a card showing Hal Reniff pitching, it corrected its mistake by issuing a card showing a portrait of Hal Reniff not pitching. This was a start. However, Topps didn't quite get that the problem with this card was not that it was not Hal Reniff or that he wasn't supposed to be pitching, but that the card was supposed to show Babe Ruth.

The mistake was in the numbering of the Hal Reniff card(s). Hal Reniff was supposed to be #159 but ended up as #139. The

Babe Ruth card #139 that showed Babe Ruth was in the right place all the time. But by having three cards with the same number Topps created a couple of nice error cards. The Reniff pitching-pose card is worth $40 in Near Mint, but is a lot scarcer than that price indicates. The Reniff portrait is more common and is an $18 card. "Babe Hits 60" is $7.

But Topps wasn't quite through with Hal Reniff. The next year's Hal Reniff card featured—you guessed it—the same portrait of Reniff used for a while in the 1962 set. One photo, one number, carefully used, could last Topps a lifetime—or at least a couple of years.

Paul's Score: 16

Kit's Score: 32

TOTAL SCORE: 48

1989 Donruss
Ken Griffey, Jr.

ne of the hardest things for a baseball-card market analyst (ha!) to do is to see a card of a good rookie come out, and get hyped, and then see the rookie make the team, and see the card get hyped further, and go up in value beyond all sense of proportion, and conclude despite all that that *the card isn't hyped at all but is actually undervalued.* The Donruss Jose Canseco rookie is not a card like that. The 1988 Donruss Gregg Jefferies is not a card like that. But the 1989 Donruss Ken Griffey, Jr., is such a card.

Ken Griffey, Jr., could be the best all-around centerfielder to come around since Willie Mays, or at least since Kirby Puckett. The comparisons to Mays come more naturally because things come so naturally to Griffey. His all-out sprint is a Jaguar glide, smooth and effortless at speed. His outfield instincts are impeccable; his hitting stroke makes Darryl Strawberry's bat-whip look crude. Griffey is more than a flash in the pan or a stab in the dark or a shooting star or a long shot or a dark horse or anything. He is the genuine article, the most very real real thing, and if each and every one of his rookie cards aren't worth a 10-spot in two years it'll be a true shock.

This is not radical, revisionist thinking here. Griffey's Donruss cards are $4 already, and have been pitched on the various baseball-card wire services for several times that. His Upper Deck card has had a $10–$12 price tag hung on it, which is excessive, and which is why the Donruss card is here and the Upper Deck card isn't. But even at $4 the Griffey card is a bargain. If he does a fraction of what he's capable of doing Griffey will leave Eric Davis and Ellis Burks and Ruben Sierra in the dust. If he does what he's capable of doing he will leave Jose Canseco behind. Even if Griffey's card is $4 now, and even if maybe 2 million of them were printed and are out there, his card is still a buy. The numbers and the odds all favor the negative these days; it's much easier to say a card is not a buy than vice versa. Ken Griffey, Jr., is the vice versa.

Paul's Score: 20

Kit's Score: 28

TOTAL SCORE: 48

1965 Topps
World Series
Game 3

very baseball card is a little bit cheesy, but the World Series cards of the early 1960s are the whole box of Velveeta. You can microwave these little jewels in two minutes and pour them over tortilla chips, and there's no way you could tell them from your average pasteurized process spread. They've got colorized black-and-white photos that take you on a game-by-game luxury motor-coach tour of the Series, and about a third of the time they actually show a colorized black-and-white scene of the game they're supposed to. The rest of the time they show whatever is sorta handy and sorta fits. The "Mantle's Clutch HR" World Series card in the 1965 set shows Mantle taking a healthy home-run cut all right, but the pitcher that Mantle hit his clutch home run off of isn't the pitcher that's pictured on this card. Maybe Topps airbrushed him out, but that's giving Topps a little too much credit in the ambition department. What's more likely is that the Topps guys had this neat shot of Mantle taking a big swing off a Cardinal pitcher and figured they probably couldn't save it until next year unless they airbrushed out Mantle and the pitcher and the stadium, so they used it.

And some collectors wonder why World Series cards aren't worth anything.

World Series cards aren't worth anything for the same reason all-star cards aren't worth anything, and the same reason we threw at you up about forty pages ago. Collectors want the real card first, and the junk can wait. It doesn't matter if a World Series card shows an unforgettable piece of cheesy airbrushed baseball history or not. A Mickey Mantle collector is going to buy the regular Mickey Mantle card first and a Mantle World Series card fourth or fifth, right after he buys a Roger Maris card and drills it full of holes, and buys a Tracy Stallard card and drills *that* full of holes.

In other words, Mickey Mantle World Series cards, like the "Mantle's Clutch HR" from the 1965 card set, are cheap cards. Not exactly. An American single like the 1961 "Mantle Slams 2 Homers" card, which actually shows him slamming one of the two homers, goes for about $20. You can almost buy two Sparky Anderson rookie cards for that, or an Ernie Banks card, or a '68 Maverick with no motor, but you can't buy much of a Mickey Mantle baseball card with that.

The '65 "Mantle's Clutch HR" card has more than doubled in price in the last two years, which shows you someone out there likes them and is willing to pay money for them, and might just be willing to pay a lot more money for them in the years ahead. Some people like Velveeta, too. You figure it out.

Paul's Score: 17

Kit's Score: 26

TOTAL SCORE: 43